PETROGLYPHS

(ROCK CARVINGS)

IN THE SUSQUEHANNA RIVER NEAR
SAFE HARBOR, PENNSYLVANIA

Pennsylvania Historical and Museum Commission
2001

ISBN 0-89271-100-0

Preface to the 2001 Edition

Donald Cadzow's 1934 publication of the "Petroglyph Book," as it has become known, has become a classic in Pennsylvania archaeology. It has been out of print for decades but it represents the best published documentation on Pennsylvanian's most spectacular petroglyphs. It is the story of how Cadzow investigated, recorded, and retrieved a unique set of petroglyphs that were being threatened by the construction of hydroelectric dams in the Safe Harbor area of the Lower Susquehanna River.

The investigation took place in the early 1930s in the midst of the depression, but also the excitement of the New Deal. The project was a major "expedition" for the Historical Commission (as it was then known) and it was all documented in a film. A pneumatic rock drill, with hoses stretched for thousands of feet, was used in recovering the petroglyphs—an impressive use of technology for the time. The project was done in cooperation with the power companies and represents the beginning of a long partnership in the region that resulted in the preservation and/or excavation of many significant archaeological sites in the Lower Susquehanna Valley. Cadzow went on to excavate many sites in the area, partly in an attempt to date the petroglyphs, and eventually he served as director of the Historical and Museum Commission.

The book contains comprehensive maps, photographs, and drawings of the petroglyphs on three small islands in the Susquehanna River—Walnut Island, Big Indian Rock, and Little Indian Rock. Plaster casts were also made of most of the larger designs. The petroglyphs on these three islands are an amazing combination of dots, lines, circles, animal tracks, abstract markings, and zoomorphic figures. They probably represent many visits and possibly the work of different cultures. These are now acknowledged to be the most numerous and elaborate set of petroglyphs in the Middle Atlantic region. These designs were undoubtedly common in prehistoric socicties and were made on wood, baskets and clothing. These types of artifacts practically never survive in the archaeological contexts of Eastern North America. Until very recently, this was the only documentation for the petroglyphs on these islands and our only direct window into the minds of the prehistoric inhabitants of the region.

The descriptions of the petroglyphs are followed by a discussion of ways that the symbols may be interpreted, and Cadzow finishes with some possible interpretations. However, Cadzow's analysis is heavily influenced by the thinking of Lewis Henry Morgan and the unilineal evolutionary theory of the 1930s. Cadzow assumes, without question, that Algonkian culture precedes the more advanced Iroquoian culture and that the simple zoomorphic designs precede the more abstract designs. Cadzow is unabashed in his statement that Walnut Island is earlier than Big and Little Indian Rock and the intervening time was marked by a "period of decadence." His comparison to Chinese writing suggests he believes that there may be some standard symbols that are similar and ancestral to all petroglyphs. Thankfully, he is probably most accurate in comparing these to Native American designs, especially Eastern Algonkian groups since they were the most frequent inhabitants of the region throughout prehistory.

When I first read *Petroglyphs* as an undergraduate thirty years ago, I considered the interpretations dated but I was thankful that they had been documented before being covered in the reservoir. I later found out that Big and Little Indian rocks are frequently uncovered when the water is lowered. I also found it fascinating to study dots, lines, and zoomorphic figures that had emerged from the minds of prehistoric peoples thousands of years ago. What do they mean? In the intervening years, a consensus has developed that most of these are Algonquin and Shenks Ferry rather than Susquehannock (Iroquoian). There is some thought that they are frequently found on the boundaries between tribal territories but there is still much research to be completed. Recently, Paul Nevin has developed improved maps of Big and Little Indian Rock and he is in the process (in 2001) of digitizing these maps. This will greatly enhance our ability to interpret the mass of lines and markings. In response to a new interest in Native American lifeways and belief systems, this will be the second printing of *Petroglyphs* by the Historical and Museum Commission. I am sure it will be enjoyed and I hope it will inspire new research into the belief systems on the Commonwealth's prehistoric inhabitants.

Kurt W. Carr
Chief of the Division of Archaeology and Protection
Bureau of Historic Preservation
Pennsylvania Historical and Museum Commission

Contents

FOREWORD

INVENTION of the first rude form of the art of writing was the first permanent step in the advance toward civilization. Until men could leave behind them a record of acquired knowledge, progress remained almost stationary except for certain arts and crafts. History was uncertain legend; science, a vague tradition; and we can safely say that man's development since the Dark Ages has sprung from the art of writing.

At one time the very idea of preserving man's thoughts and deeds was considered a miracle, and very often attributed to some divine inspiration. A knowledge of writing during certain periods of the world's history has been considered dangerous, for it was used in the beginning primarily as the tool of priests and magicians. As time rolled on ordinary man made crude marks or symbols to identify his property or to recall useful information. Very often notched sticks, knotted cords, or certain objects associated with the occasion or deed to be remembered were placed in bundles with a skin covering and carefully guarded.

As writing developed it passed through three main stages, pictographic, ideographic and phonetic, toward the alphabetic. Our own English alphabet is a mixture derived from the Egyptian hieroglyphic through the hieratic, Phoenician, Hebrew, Ancient Greek, Latin, and perhaps other sources until a group of common signs emerged.

Passing over the first stages of mnemonic symbolism, still shrouded in the mists of antiquity, we reach the form of thought writing which seeks to convey ideas by means of signs or marks suggestive or imitative of the object or idea in mind. These were made upon a variety of objects such as bone, bark, skins, copper, gourds, wood, and stone. Textile fabrics, beads, feathers, quills, and hair worked in a variety of ways and designs also were used for records. Most of these objects exposed to the elements disintegrated and we have to look to stone for our early writing.

Scientists are not absolutely certain of the ancient relation between what we now call the Old World and the New. The struggle toward civilization was similar, regardless of location, and some reached the goal sooner than others. Picture signs were employed by most peoples, but it is chiefly to the American Indians we must look for knowledge of their use and purpose, since among them alone, to the best of our knowledge, pictographs still can be translated and are found in full and significant use today.

From the earliest known form of picture writing the American Indians progressed ideographically to an expression of abstract ideas. In many ways the most important and interesting mnemonic records still being used are those of the secret Midewin Society of the Central Algonquin (1). By means of figures etched upon birch bark certain ideas are conveyed to the mind and used in ceremonies. The songs and rituals of the society can be interpreted by initiates who have paid the high priests of the fraternity for the knowledge.

Because of the use of pictographic devices by the great secret fraternities among the American Indians, they, as a general rule, are uncommunicative concerning the possible meaning of ancient petroglyphs*. These records are found in a variety of places—sea and river-washed boulders, glacier-polished rocks, in caves, and on canyon walls in various parts of North America. They are not idle scrawls made to gratify a passing whim. In their day many of them played an important part in the social organizations of the tribes. Their significance among most students in the past has always been believed to be more local than general; they have been classified as individual and not tribal or national. Modern anthropologists, however, with their knowledge of the distribution of the great Indian linguistic stocks and social organizations, are beginning to believe that many ancient petroglyphs have a wide range and a much deeper significance.

Detailed information concerning the translation of North American petroglyphs is not available. Scientists have hesitated to delve into this little known field of research as contemporary data in most places cannot be found. Industrial expansion, however, is forcing attention to this field. Along the rivers great dams are being built and the pictographs, our sole surviving examples of very early American graphic art, are being buried beneath the waters. The natural erosion of stone in many places has been the means of destroying many records, and Indian "picture rocks" are but a memory in many localities.

To date no explanatory key has ever been discovered gener-

* The name petroglyph was first applied to rock writings by Dr. Richard Andree in his work *Ethnographische Parallelem Und Vergleiche*, Stuttgart, 1878.

ally applicable to Indian pictographic symbols. Types and tendencies have been classified in certain regions although no general application of interpreting laws can be made outside of certain Algonkian, Siouan and Pueblo groups. The fanciful hypotheses formed in the past about the Susquehanna River pictographs in Pennsylvania have been discarded. Many pictographs on the lower river were destroyed by the backwater of the Holtwood and Conowingo hydro-electric dams. Those in the area between Safe Harbor and Washington Borough herein described would have been destroyed if it had not been for the Pennsylvania Historical Commission and the officials of the Safe Harbor Water Power Corporation of Baltimore. The generosity of the latter company in supplying men and equipment for the recording and removal of the petroglyphs in the area to be covered with water has no parallel in the history of anthropology in this country.

The writer takes this opportunity to thank the following persons for their generous and whole-hearted cooperation in all that was accomplished at Safe Harbor during 1930-1932: Mr. Frederic A. Godcharles, Milton, Pennsylvania; Miss Frances Dorrance, Wilkes-Barre, Pennsylvania; Messrs. J. E. Aldred and Charles E. Clarke, New York City; Messrs. John A. Walls, Roland Bortner, E. J. Monaghan and George Settar, Baltimore, Maryland; Messrs. H. E. Whitney and S. Burns, Safe Harbor, Pennsylvania; Mr. David H. Landis, Windon, Pennsylvania; Mr. R. C. Steinmetz, Harrisburg, Pennsylvania; Mr. Samuel Pennypacker, II, Germantown, Pennsylvania; Mr. Frank Thomas Siebert, Jr., Philadelphia, Pennsylvania; Mr. John Joseph Stoudt, Allentown, Pennsylvania; and Dr. Arthur C. Parker, Rochester, New York.

DONALD A. CADZOW, *Archaeologist*
Pennsylvania Historical Commission

PLATE I

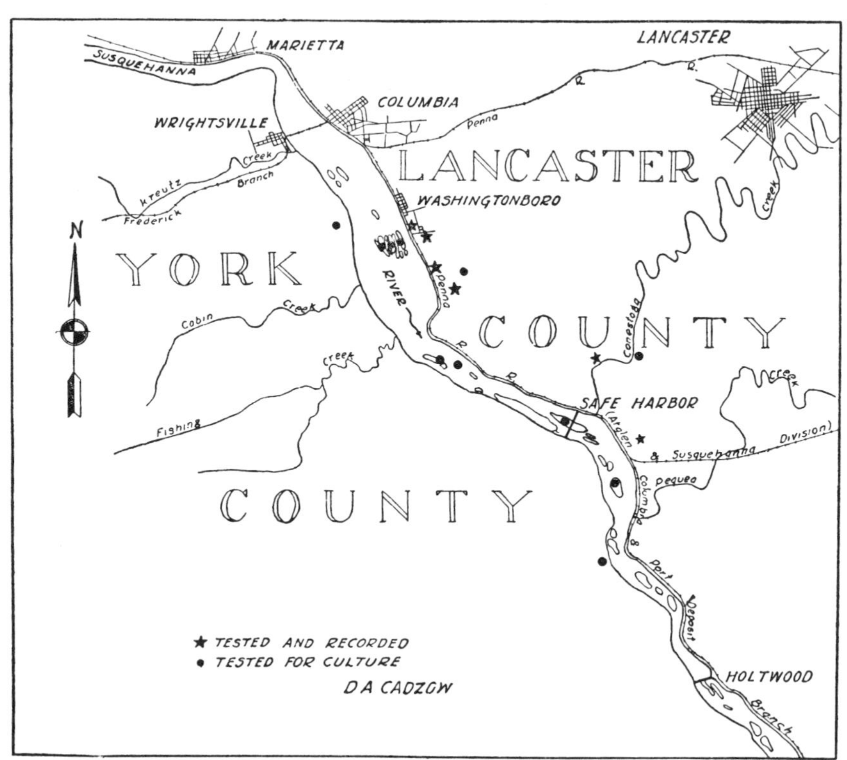

ARCHAEOLOGICAL SURVEY, 1930-1932

Petroglyphs in the Susquehanna River Near Safe Harbor

Man throughout the ages has ever shown a desire to perpetuate his history. Most permanent but least intelligible of his records are the petroglyphs or rock inscriptions near his ancient habitations.

For many years the petroglyphs on the lower Susquehanna River in Pennsylvania and Maryland have been known to scientists. In 1871 the first accurate reference to them was made in the transactions of the Anthropological Institute of New York. In 1889 Dr. W. J. Hoffman visited the region and made sketches of the petroglyphs and declared them to be of Algonkian origin. At approximately the same time, Professor P. Frazer, Jr. investigated the same records observed by Dr. Hoffman and wrote the following account concerning them:

"In addition to the natural causes of obliteration it is a pity to have to record the vandalism of some of the visitors to the locality who have thought it an excellent practical joke to cut spurious figures alongside and sometimes over the top of those made by the Indians. Parts of the connected story to which they are related have been separated and the record destroyed. Others have cut their initials or full names in the rocks, the correct deciphering of which leads to obscurity itself." (2)

The writings described by Frazer and Hoffman are located on what is called Big and Little Indian Rocks about one-half mile below the new power dam at Safe Harbor (plates I-II). Since 1889 the vandals continued their work of destroying the figures pecked upon the rocks by the Indians, and when the place was first visited by the Commission expedition on April 5, 1930, we found such things as a "dove of peace" with an olive branch in its mouth chiseled into the rocks, together with initials dating from 1780 to 1930. Vandalism has destroyed many of the original records and has led to a local belief that the figures are not of Indian origin. The expedition was told confidentially by responsible people that the State was wasting time and money in investigation since all the inscriptions were spurious. Certain figures, however, indicated that if they were frauds, their makers had considerable knowledge of Indian customs and ceremonies.

Big and Little Indian Rocks were in no immediate danger and it was decided to concentrate the efforts of the group upon finding the records in the ten mile area above the mouth of Conestoga Creek near which the great concrete wall of the new dam was being built across the river.

Mr. David Landis of Windon, Lancaster County, had reported to Miss Frances Dorrance, secretary of the Historical Commission, that he had found writings upon the rocks in the river in the area we intended to explore. He very kindly consented to point out the writings to the members of the expedition, and on April 8, 1930, we poled our boat through the swift water in the area between the high hills above Safe Harbor and started a search for records that kept us busy for the next two years.

The first important group of writings was located about three miles above Safe Harbor on Walnut Island, which had received its name from a fine stand of walnut trees that had once flourished upon it. The trees were cut down by an early settler named Neff, who rented the island for farming from John Musser. The difficulty of transporting crops from this isolated spot, surrounded by swift water, made the farming project impractical and the island was abandoned. Subsequently, another settler moved in and decided to build a mill on the upper end of the island. After digging a race the project was abandoned. The race, however, offered a ready passage for the spring floods which tore away a considerable section of the island on the York county side, and, aided by previous erosion caused by the farming project, exposed a long section of the waterworn out-cropping of mica-schist. Upon these exposed smooth rocks Mr. Landis pointed out the first of the ancient writings.

Within the next few weeks twenty-one groups of writings were found upon this island and they were unquestionably of an entirely different period than those on Big and Little Indian Rocks a few miles down the river (plates III-IV).

A close investigation of the formation upon which the writings were found revealed that the mica-schist had veins of white quartzite running through it. The dip in the rocks was almost vertical and many of them were fractured. This presented a real problem if they were to be removed, so it was decided not to attempt to take them out until a complete record could be taken in situ.

PLATE II

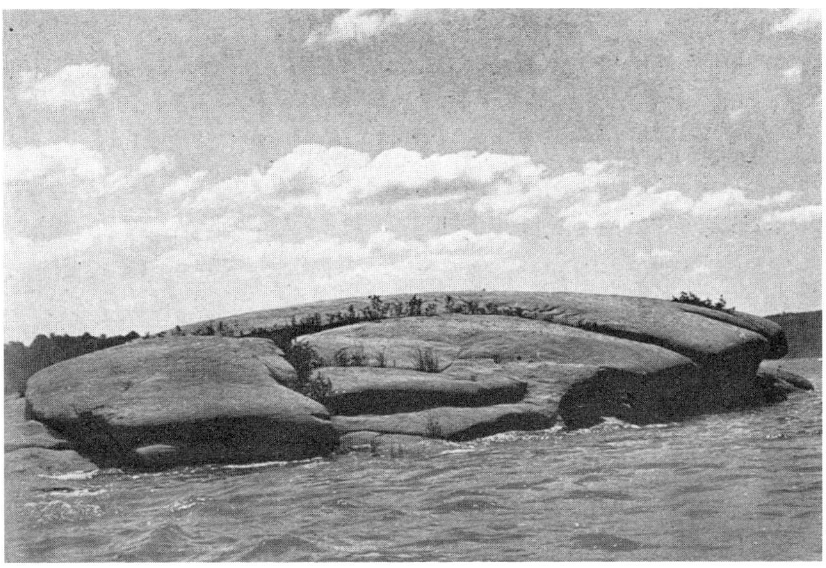

Big Indian Rock in the Susquehanna River Near Safe Harbor

A

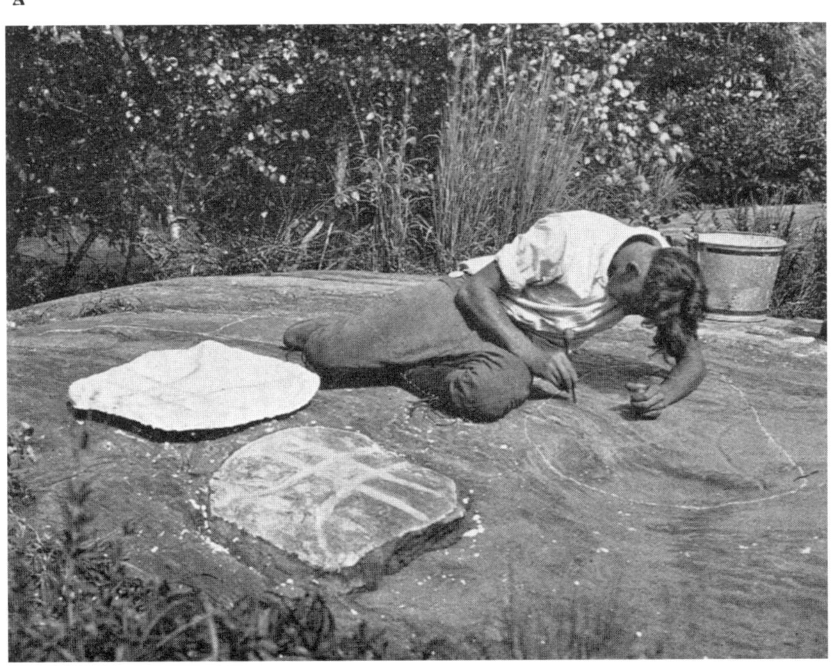

Making Plaster Molds on Walnut Island

PLATE III

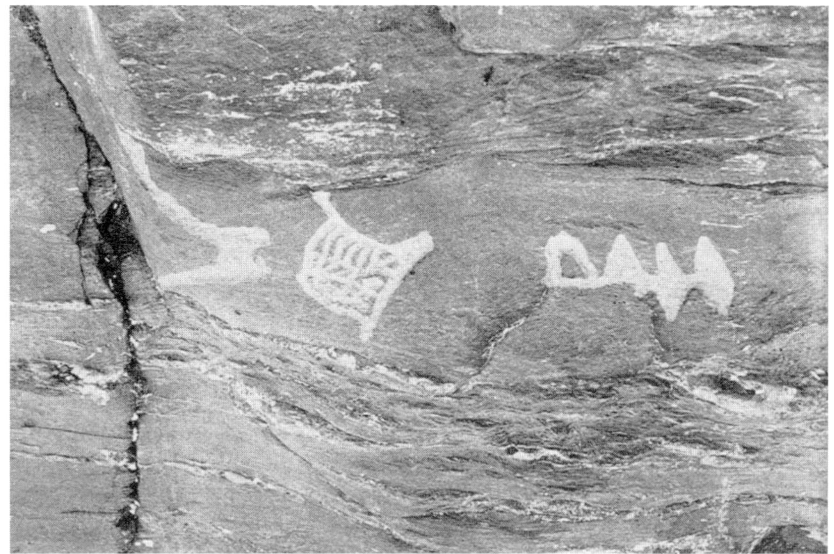

Petroglyphs on Walnut Island

PLATE IV

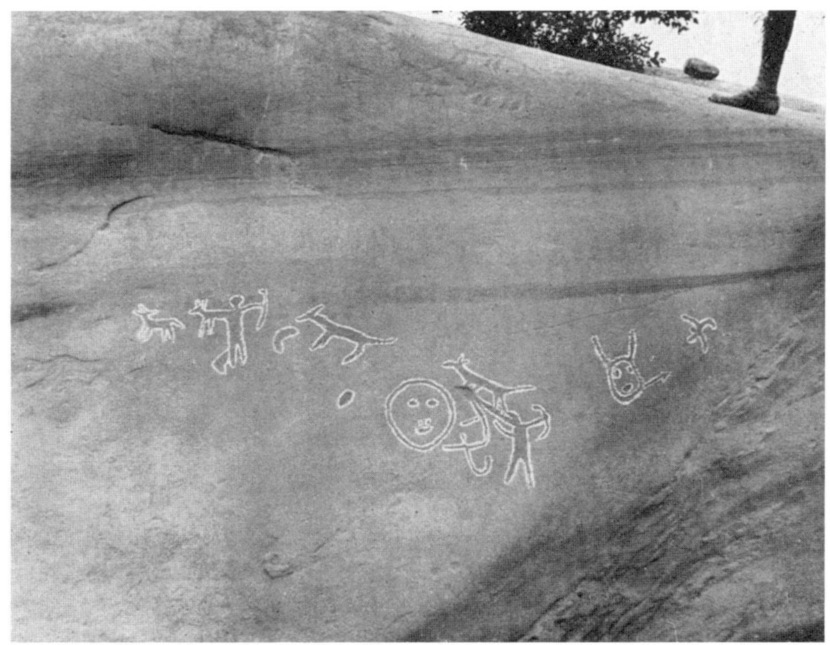

Petroglyphs on Little Indian Rock

Arrangements were made with Dr. Arthur Parker, Director of the Rochester Museum of Arts and Sciences, to allow Mr. Linneaus Duncan, expert preparator and technician on his staff, to come to Safe Harbor for the purpose of making plaster molds of the writings before any attempt was made to remove them. While waiting for Mr. Duncan, four workmen were loaned to us by the Power Company and the task of clearing trails through the jungle-like second growth of the island was started. Temporary headquarters were established on high ground and supplies necessary to carry on the work were obtained. On April 24, 1930, Mr. Henry K. Deisher and Mr. Eugene M. Gardner of the State Museum staff reported, and the task of trying to unravel the Indian history of this part of Pennsylvania began in earnest.

The most important undertaking after the trails were cut was to attempt to establish an occupation contemporary with the petroglyphs. Test trenches were carried across the island and the strata carefully studied. We did not realize at the time how far afield this work would take us nor that many new pages of Pennsylvania pre-history would be written before the expedition left Safe Harbor.

The archaeological excavations revealed the fact that the lower end of the island had been washed innumerable times by floods which had deposited silt to varying depths. This, of course, made it impossible to establish any conclusive evidence of the occupation of man. The upper end of the island where a cellar had been dug for a farm house revealed a temporary white settlement near the surface of the ground, but below this were indications of Indian habitation, such as fragments of pottery vessels and stone arrowheads, all of Algonkian type.

One small crew of men was put to work excavating the soil on the lower end of the island, near the finest pictographs, in an effort to check the story of the earth having been washed away, revealing these ancient markings. One important group was found several feet beneath the surface. This may perhaps indicate that the soil upon the lower end of the island covered many more records. It was however, an impossible task to remove the thousands of tons of earth and we had to be satisfied with the exposed writings.

Mr. John Funk, of Washington borough, an expert river man, joined our party on April 29th. With Mr. Funk as pilot we set out to examine every large rock and explore, archaeologically, every island in the area to be covered by the backwater of the dam (plates V-VI). On Big Island in the center of the river, opposite the town of Washington Borough, evidence of a large Indian site was found, but, as on the lower end of Walnut Island, succeeding floods had destroyed all evidence in situ. Recent deposits of river coal, some at a depth of four or five feet, indicated heavy floods within recent years. While this exploring expedition on the river did not discover important archaeological evidence, it did find some unusually interesting petroglyphs on the Lancaster side not far from Creswell railroad station.

On May 1, 1930, Mr. Duncan reported at Safe Harbor and the task of recording the petroglyphs in plaster was started. First, it was decided to make scale drawings of each figure in place with its position carefully noted. After this was done, plaster molds were made of each of the rocks upon which the writings occurred. These molds were poured in sections, each carefully marked so that we could assemble them later and produce casts exactly like the original rocks. The fact that 188 plaster sections were made during the summer provides some idea as to the magnitude of this task. Each mold was backed by strips of burlap and carefully dried before being taken to the laboratory at Safe Harbor.

At the beginning of the work, barrels of plaster had to be brought to the island in a small boat through the dangerous stretches of swift water on the York County side of the river. The first lot of molds was taken from the island the same way, but as this road proved to be too rough for the transportation of friable plaster, other arrangements had to be made. A channel leading down through the rapids to Safe Harbor was finally discovered, and, when the Power Company presented a heavy dory to the expedition, and the Indian Motor Company donated an outboard motor, the problem of transporting the molds was solved.

While the work of preserving the petroglyphs in plaster was being carried on, the archaeological field party finished its task on the small islands nearby and started to investigate a large island near Washington borough, called House Island, upon which some indications of Indian occupancy had been reported. The same conditions were found there as upon Big Island, Wal-

PLATE V

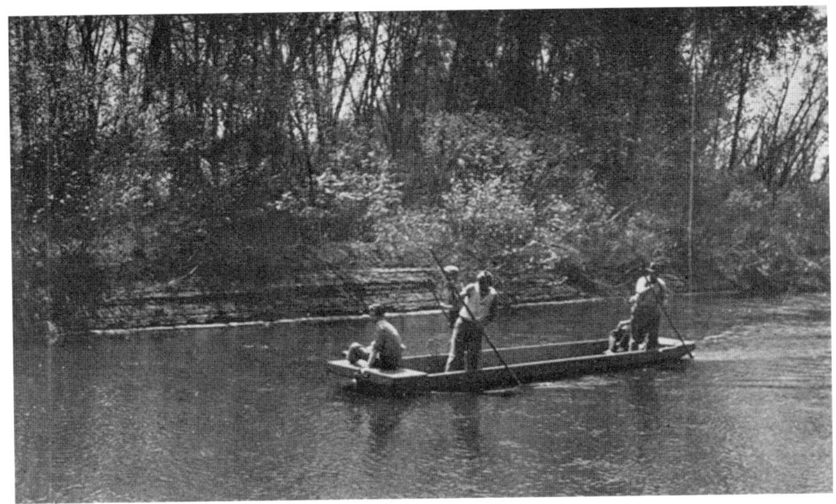

Exploring the Islands in the Area to Be Covered by the Backwater of the Safe Harbor Dam

PLATE VI

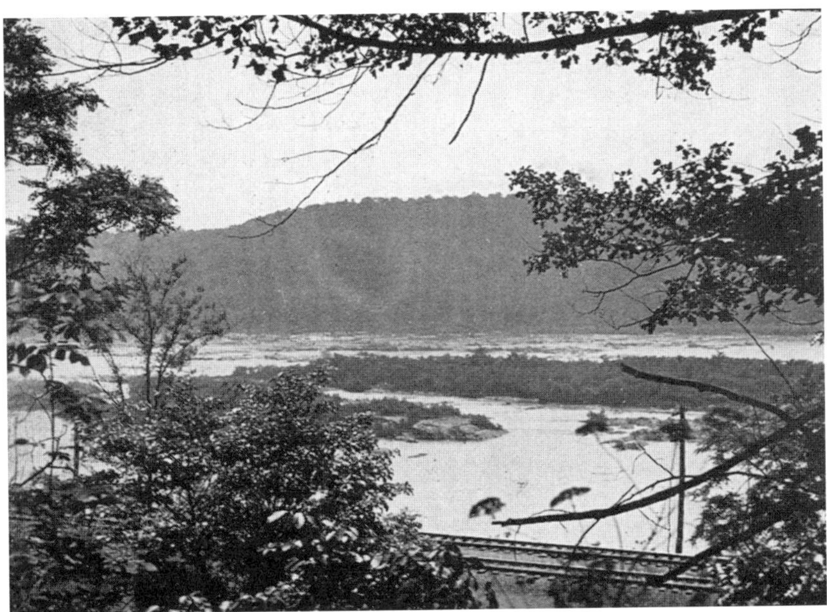

Walnut Island From the Lancaster County Side of the River

PLATE VII

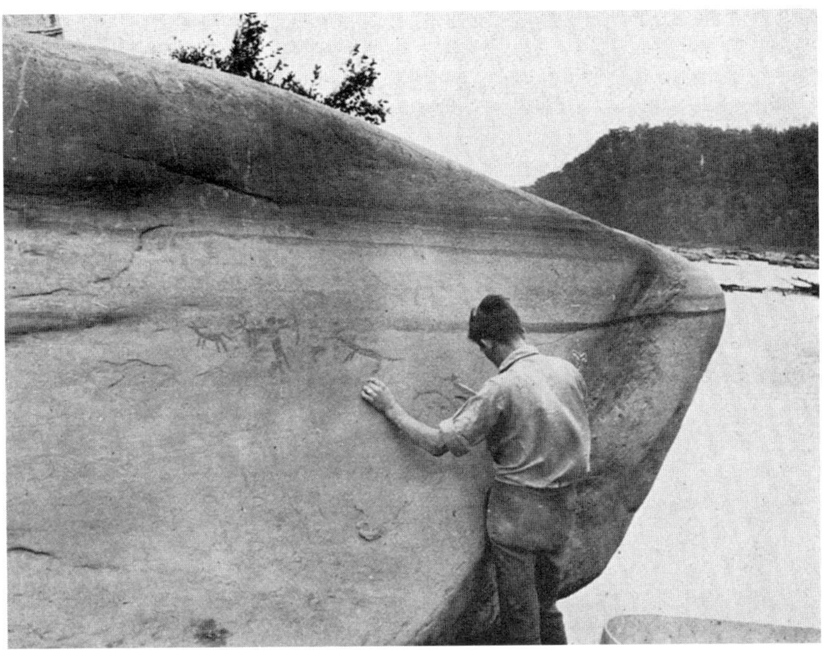

Charting Petroglyphs Usually Covered by Water in the Basin of the Holtwood Dam

PLATE VIII

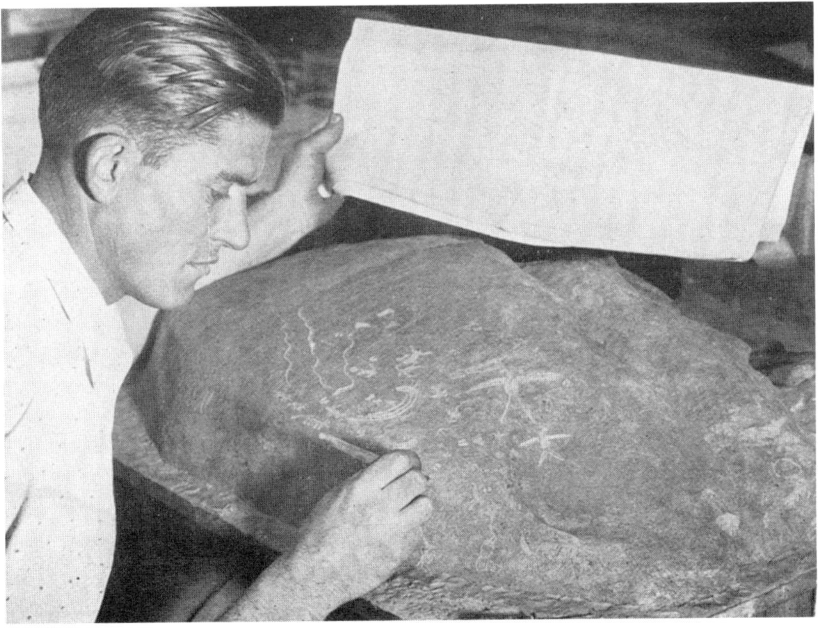

Mr. Duncan Making a Scale Model of Little Indian Rock

nut Island and others in the area; all archaeological records, in situ, had been destroyed by the river.

The exploration party had proved that it was impossible to secure accurate stratification in the area reached by the great floods that at one time swept down the Susquehanna. The soil had been thoroughly stirred to varying depths except upon a few high sections on the large islands, and while occasional specimens could be found, necessary information as to cultural strata was missing.

Mr. Funk pointed out large groups of rocks in the river that within the past fifty years had been small islands and also islands that had been nothing but rocks. Undoubtedly, the great power of Susquehanna floods was known to the early inhabitants of the valley and they selected their permanent village sites accordingly. It was, however, important that the expedition explore the area to be covered by water very thoroughly so this work was carried on until late in July. At that time the party moved on to the mainland where astonishing and unusual archaeological discoveries were made which will be described later in this series.

The mechanical work of reproducing the pictographic records on Walnut Island in plaster was being carried on very ably by Mr. Duncan and his assistants, and the molds were accumulating rapidly in our laboratory at Safe Harbor. Time was now available to study the effects that the new dam would have upon the records on Big and Little Indian Rocks. For many years they had been partially covered by the backwater from Holtwood dam, ten miles down river. It was finally decided to make molds of all the authentic figures upon these two rocks, together with scale models and charts (plate VIII). This work was finished late in the fall of 1930, and to prevent further erosion of the rapidly disappearing figures, the rocks were treated with preservatives.

By the latter part of October when cold weather set in, all the authentic petroglyphs in the area to be covered by the water were set in plaster and carried to the State Museum in Harrisburg. The unusually dry summer had facilitated the work and made it possible for us to record many of the figures covered in the Holtwood basin.

The rapidly increasing archaeological collection from the mainland meant many days of laboratory work. This was carried on by Mr. William House and Mr. Elvin Herr of the engineering staff of the Power Company, after the assistants from the State Museum and the men from various colleges in the Commonwealth, who had been helping us, had left.

During the winter of 1930-31 plans were made to remove the rocks upon which the writings occurred from the area to be covered by water. Several experiments were carried out and preparations were made to start the work as soon as the ice moved. Nothing could be lost now by an attempt to lift the rocks themselves out of the river bed. In April a two and one-half ton compressor was borrowed from the Safe Harbor Company, together with several hundred feet of two-inch pipe and rubber air hose. This material was hauled to a point on the mainland near Walnut Island. Then began the task of laying an air line from the compressor to the petroglyphs, a distance of some 3,700 feet. The first problem was to cross about 350 feet of very swift water. In about two weeks, however, the line was completed and ready for operation. The swift water had been crossed by means of cable stretched from the shore to the island from which an air hose was suspended, and the rest of the distance was covered by pipe (plate IX).

On the end of the air line a pneumatic rock drill was attached, so that once the line was completed all that was necessary was to begin the actual drilling. The rocks were carefully marked into sections of varying shapes and sizes dictated by the necessity of keeping down weight and at the same time preserving the original groups of pictographs as nearly as possible. Some were circular in shape, some irregular, while one was more than nine feet long and about one foot wide (plate (XI).

Several experiments were made before the actual work was started upon the pictographs (plate X). It was finally decided that the best method was to drill two-inch holes completely around the figures, and then with a paving breaker broach the drilling and chip away the surrounding rock. After this was done, holes were drilled on a plane with the surface and the rock finally jarred loose (plate (X-B). To our great surprise very few of the writings were broken apart by this method of removal. The mica-schist proved to be unusually hard and the veins of quartzite helped to hold the rock together.

Every rock drilled had to be moved by hand as it was impossible to bring heavy machinery through the rapids to the island. Some of the pieces of rock weighed hundreds of pounds and had to be moved a considerable distance to a safe landing place for the dory. Then they were carried down through the rapids to Safe Harbor.

Using the same methods as on Walnut Island, the records found near Creswell Station were removed and saved from destruction. This latter group, however, had to be boated up through the rapids to a landing near the station and carried by truck from that point to Safe Harbor. In all, sixty-eight sections were drilled from the surfaces of Walnut Island and Creswell Rock and removed to safety. While all this hard work was going on along the river, the mainland archaeological party maintained a continuous search for human evidence contemporary with the Walnut Island, Creswell, and Big and Little Indian writings. No positive evidence of the people who made the writings upon the rocks above the dam was found.

Walnut Island Group

Chart 1

Petroglyphs in the Safe Harbor area can be divided into two ideographic groups: (1) conventionalized and (2) actual representations of objects and abstract ideas.

The petroglyphs found upon the rocks of Walnut Island are conventionalized and belong in group one. Their meanings are obscured since only the most essential points of the figures are indicated, and in this form they are not recognizable as objective portraitures. Erosion has destroyed parts of many of the original figures and because of their lack of character it may never be possible to interpret them with any degree of certainty. We can, however, use them as comparatively important indications of the grades of culture reached by human beings whose antiquity is not yet measurable to us by computation of years or even centuries. If the people who made the figures on Walnut Island used zoömorphic characters in recording their first efforts at graphic art, as they probably did, a desire to save labor later led them to use only the lines necessary to show what was meant. The thought expressed was supposed to be known to everyone interested, just as the combination of the three Latin character d-o-g signifies a dog to us in English.

In taking up our study of the conventionalized petroglyphs we have been forced to take a hypothetical position in regard to comparative interpretation of the figures. Every known system of writing has begun with rude pictures of objects. These pictures, more or less conventionalized, were gradually assumed as the representatives of words, and afterward became the symbols of elementary sounds. Because of this widespread use of ideograms and the lack of nearby contemporary data, our comparisons must be international and national rather than local.*

The first point that arises in the examination of a petroglyph is to determine, if possible, by what group of people it was made; the second, to make comparisons with writings of similar type or style. This is done with the idea in mind of tracing migrations or showing human development along similar lines. The most ancient forms of writing, to the best of our knowledge, are known as Hittite, Elamite, and Cretan. We are, perhaps, going very far afield when we compare our conventional-

*Writing began with ideograms which afterward developed into phonograms.

ized petroglyphs of Pennsylvania with the untranslated writings made by the Hittites of Asia Minor and northern Syria. These people lived prior to 1000 B. C. and left many highly conventionalized petroglyphs upon the rocks near Cappadocia, Lydia, and Lycaonia. In some respects the Cypriote graphic art, which, we believe, had its true origin with the Hittites, resembles that of the unknown ancient Pennsylvanians. We do not mean to convey the idea that the Hittites or Cypriotes migrated to the Susquehanna Valley. The comparison is made to show that people may partially develop along somewhat similar lines remote from each other in what might be entirely different eras.

There is a wide gap in the continuity of the development of our alphabet. The Phoenicians have been credited with its invention, but most modern authorities believe they developed it from the elements of more ancient known systems of writings and characters used by their contemporaries. Our writing has reached the alphabetic stage, yet we still continue to employ a considerable number of phonographic and ideographic signs.

According to Grotefend, several Roman numerals now in use are ancient ideograms. That the digits one, two and three, may be regarded as pictures of the fingers is implied by their name, and it is most probable that "V" was at first a picture of the fork of the hand with the fingers collected and the thumb apart so that "VV" or "X" represents the two hands, while "IV" and "VI" would be a picture of the hand with the subtraction or addition of a finger.

If the history of any one of our alphabetic symbols is traced back, it will be found to resolve itself ultimately into the conventionalized picture of some object. In spite of long-continued usage during so many centuries, modern letters retain in almost every instance manifest features derived from the primitive picture from which they descended.

The great systems of writing are of such antiquity that their history has to be explained to a great extent by the aid of conjecture and analogy. Hence the rudimentary forms of picture writing, such as those found near Safe Harbor, are of considerable interest and value, inasmuch as they help to throw light on the earlier stages of the development of graphic symbols.

An unknown interval in the history of writing just preceded the development of our present graphic art. The time that elapsed between the recording of the figures found on Walnut Island and the later ones upon Big and Little Indian Rocks apparently marked a period of decadence.

There are many mysteries still to be solved about the antiquity and the development of man and his migrations.

A very close analogy can be made between the writings of the ancient Chinese and those found on Walnut Island. Several learned Oriental scholars have examined these figures and have interpreted their meaning in Chinese. This is to be expected, for the Chinese use from 20,000 to 40,000 syllabic characters ranging from ideographic, figurative-combined, indicative, reversed, metaphoric to phonetic. In a study of Chinese characters we find the most notable instance of a graphic system which never succeeded in advancing far beyond the rudimentary steps of conventionalized picture writing. The early processes in the development of conventional picture writing may, therefore, be studied to advantage by comparison with the Chinese. With their wide range of symbols certain characters evolved would be similar to those of the early Americans. The primary fault in the hypothetical identification of these symbols resembling Chinese characters is that without presenting a detailed study no account can be taken of historical variations of Chinese writings. Some of the pictographs bear a resemblance, perhaps fortuitous, to some modern Chinese forms; others, to ancient ideograms. The following identifications were obtained from Chinese scholars who were not specialized in ancient epigraphy. Scientifically, their interpretations can be presented only as guesses, and they support no definite conclusions.

Figures 22, 29 and 41 are the Chinese symbols for "well of water." A similar design, without the dot in the center and with the horizontal lines straight instead of curved at the bottom, was used among the Arikara, Mandan, and Hidatsa American Indians to signify that one whose person or property this figure appears upon has successfully defended himself against the enemy in battle.

Among the Ojibway Indians, one of the largest tribes of Algonkian stock, whose range was formerly along both shores of Lake Huron and Lake Superior, extending across what is now Minnesota and North Dakota, a similar design without the dot, and with the lower ends of both vertical lines drawn out either to the right or left, signified that the person to whom

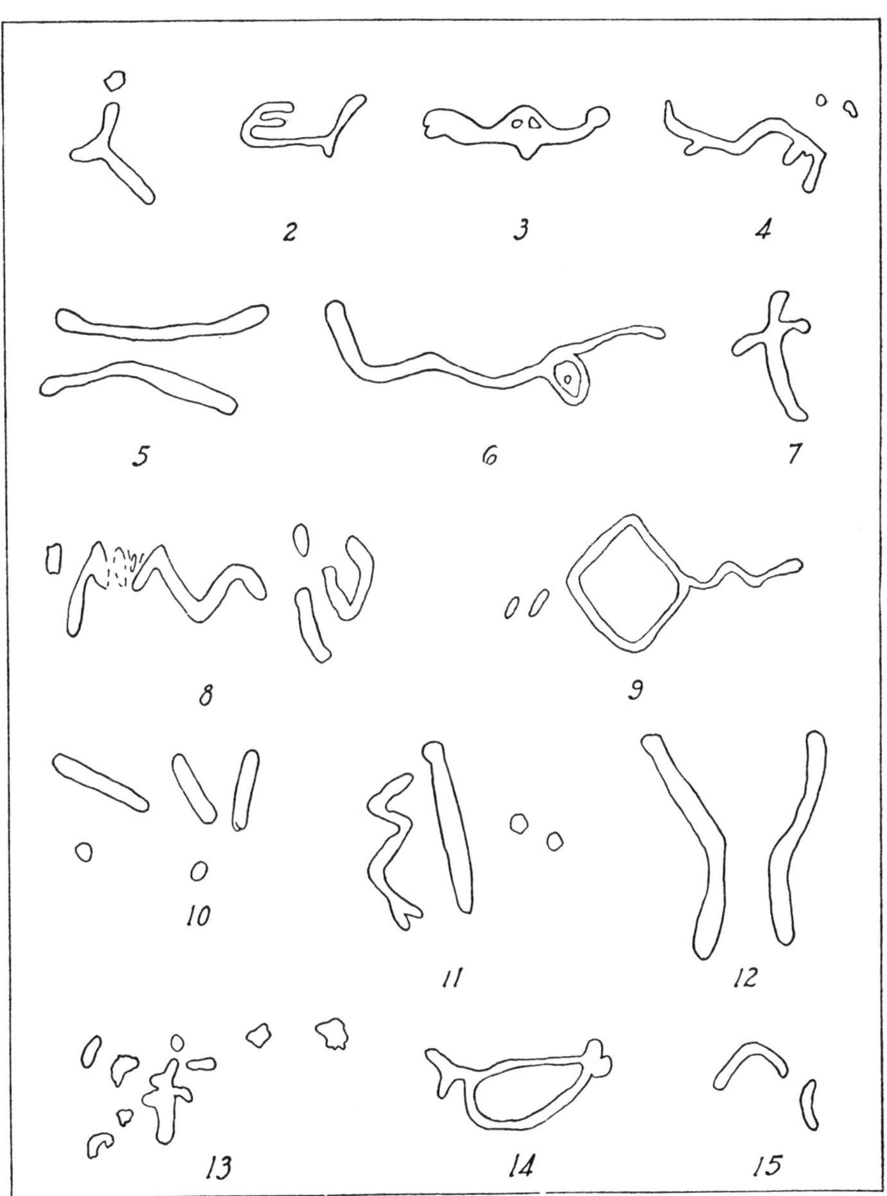
2
3
4
5
6
7
8
9
10
11
12
13
14
15

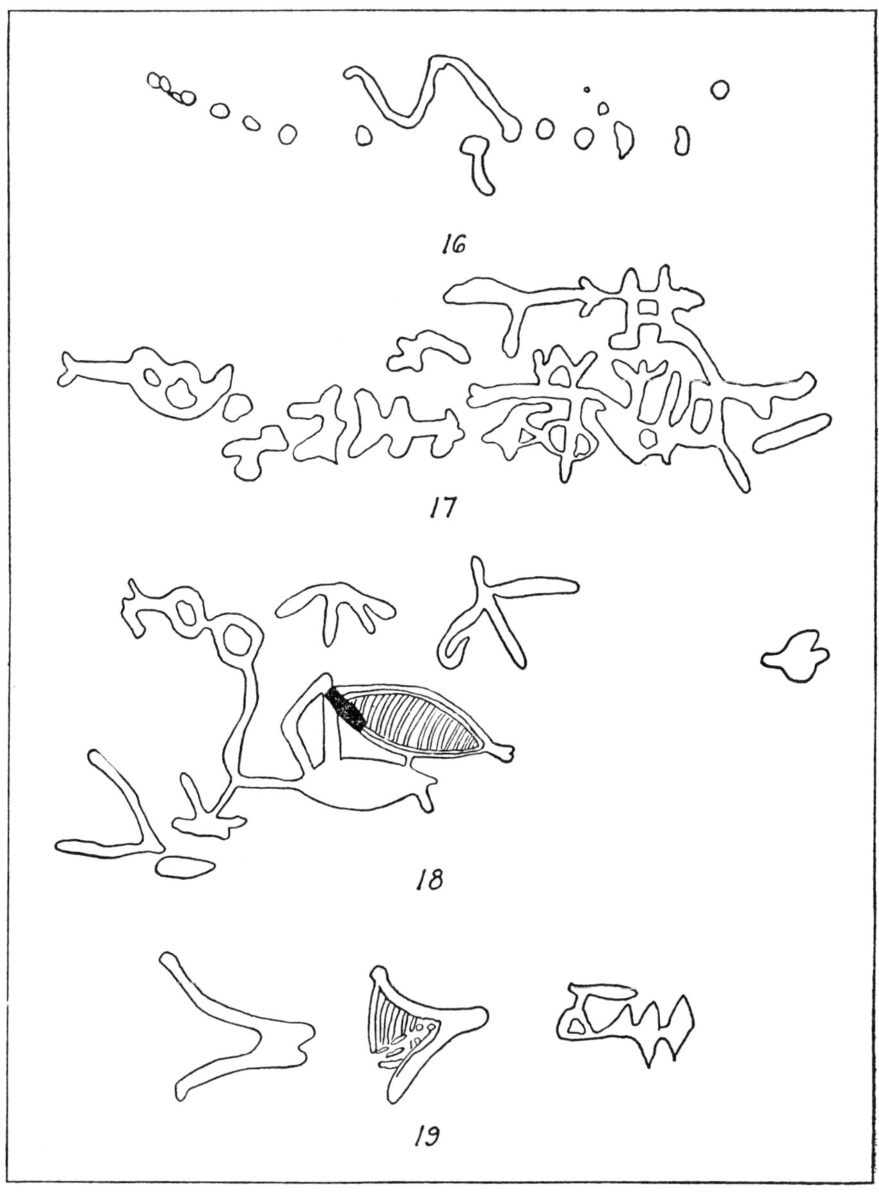
16
17
18
19

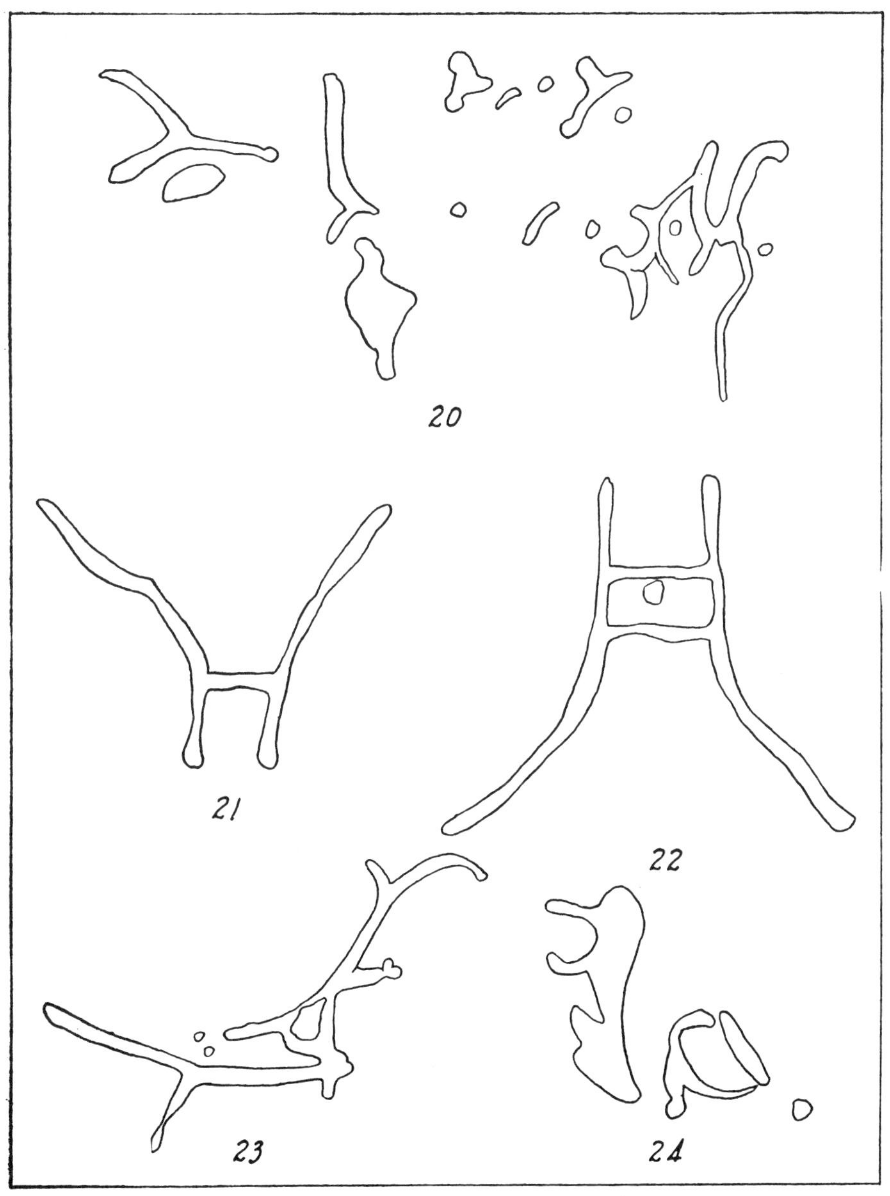
20
21
22
23
24

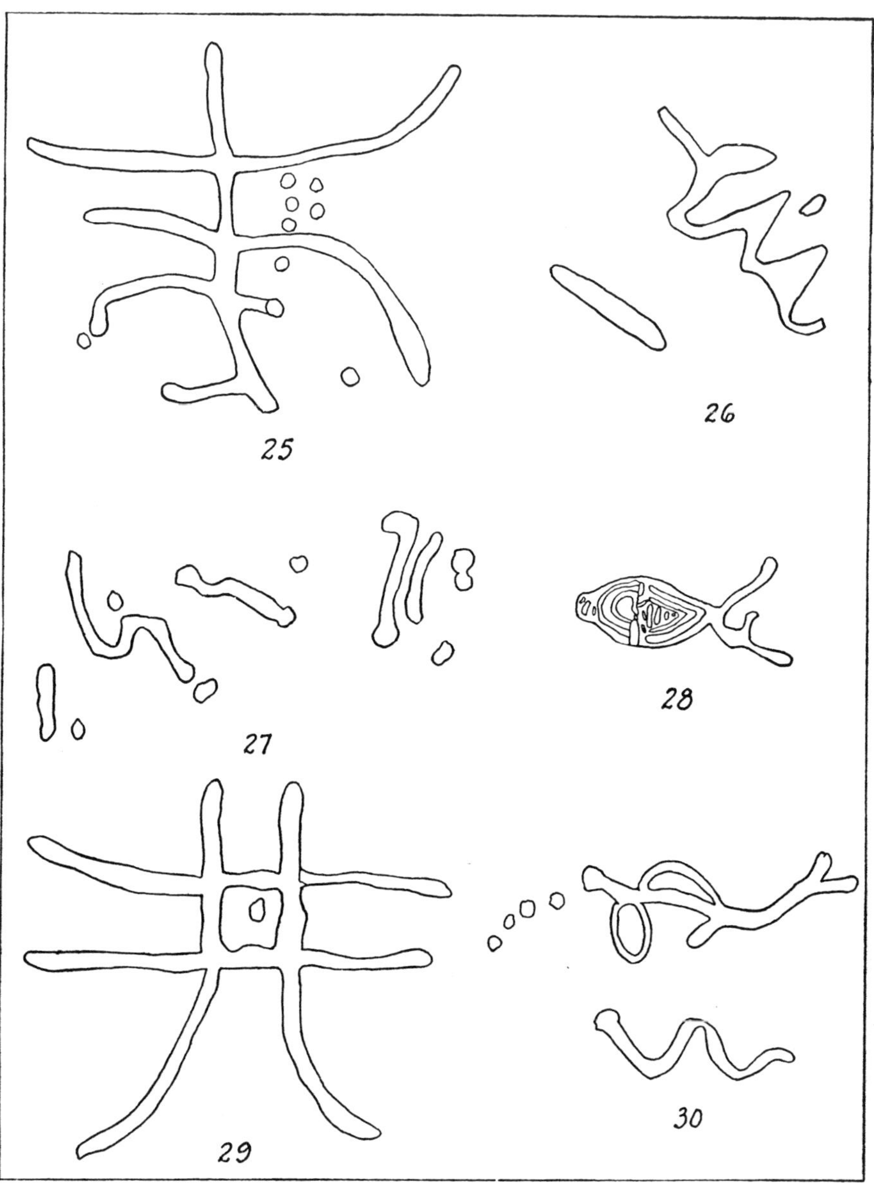
25
26
27
28
29
30

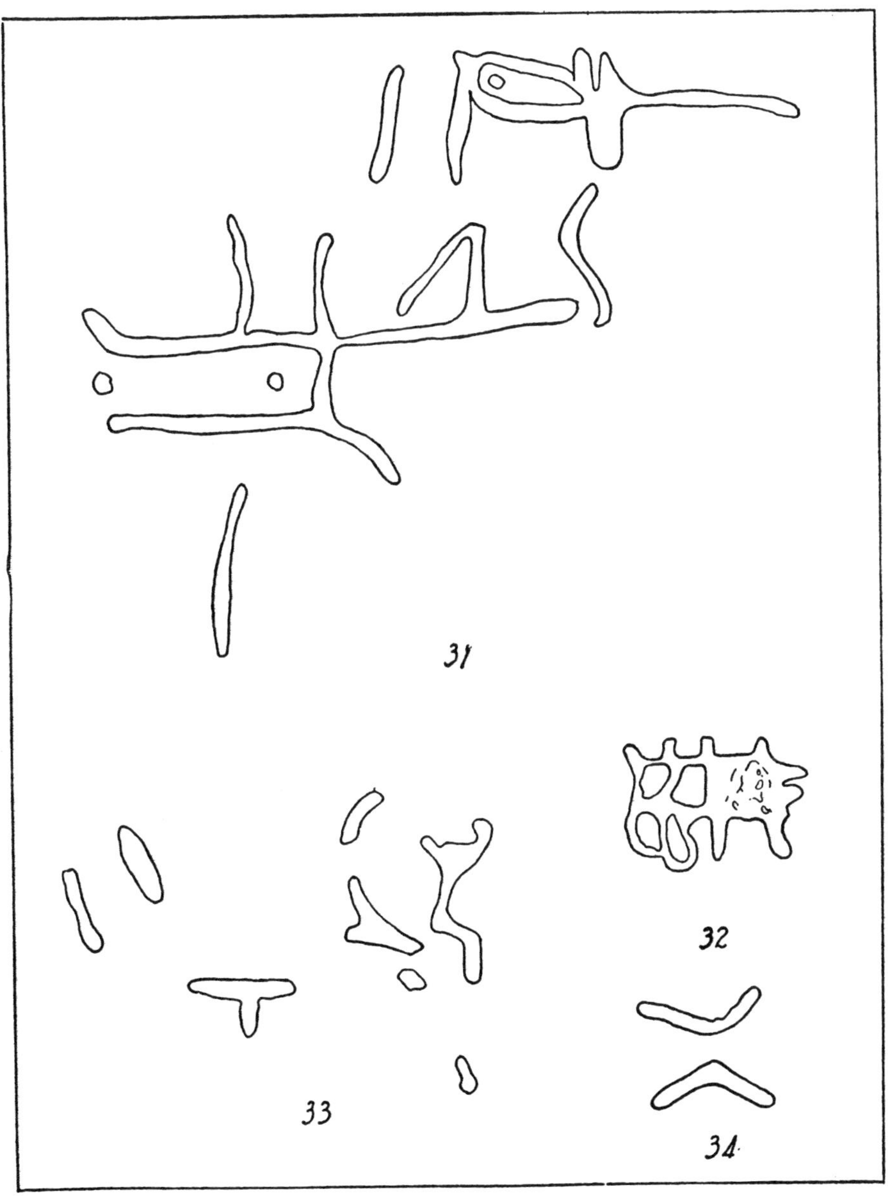
31
32
33
34

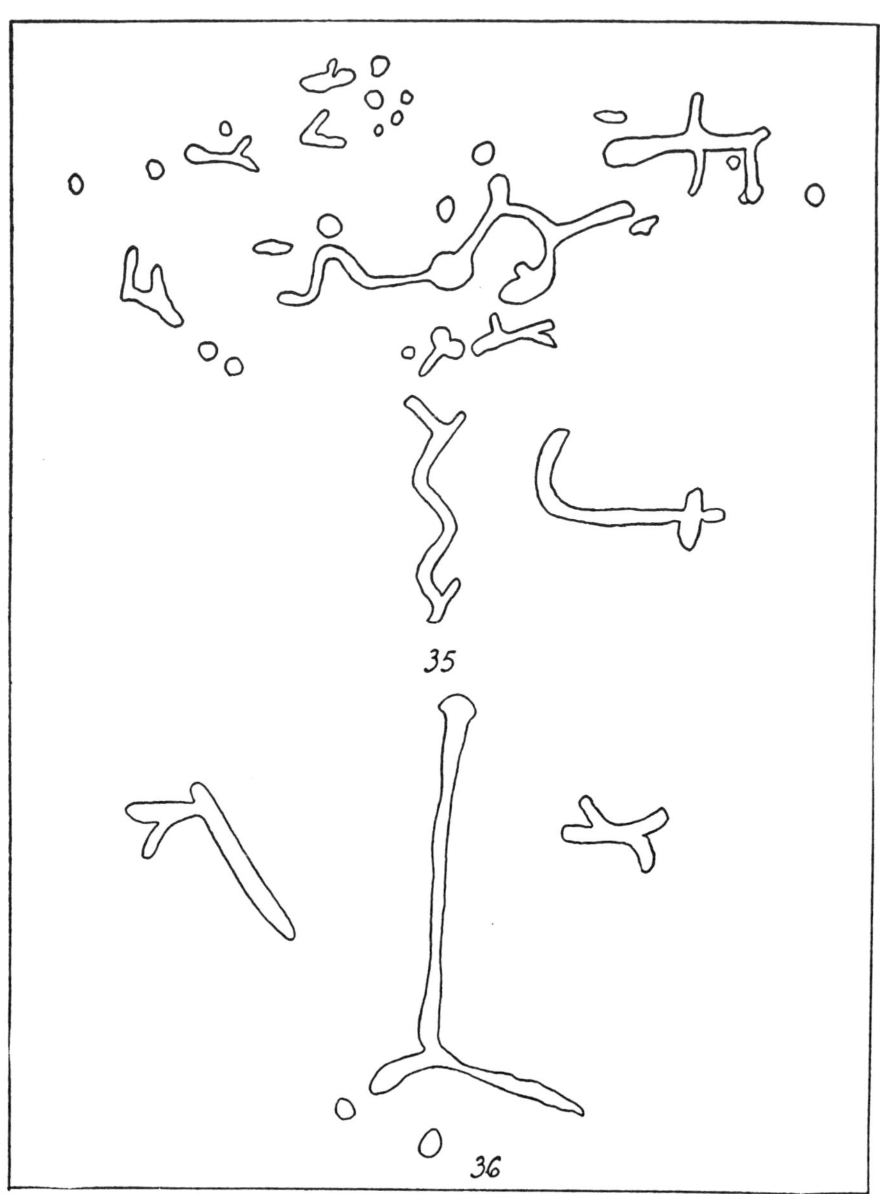
35
36

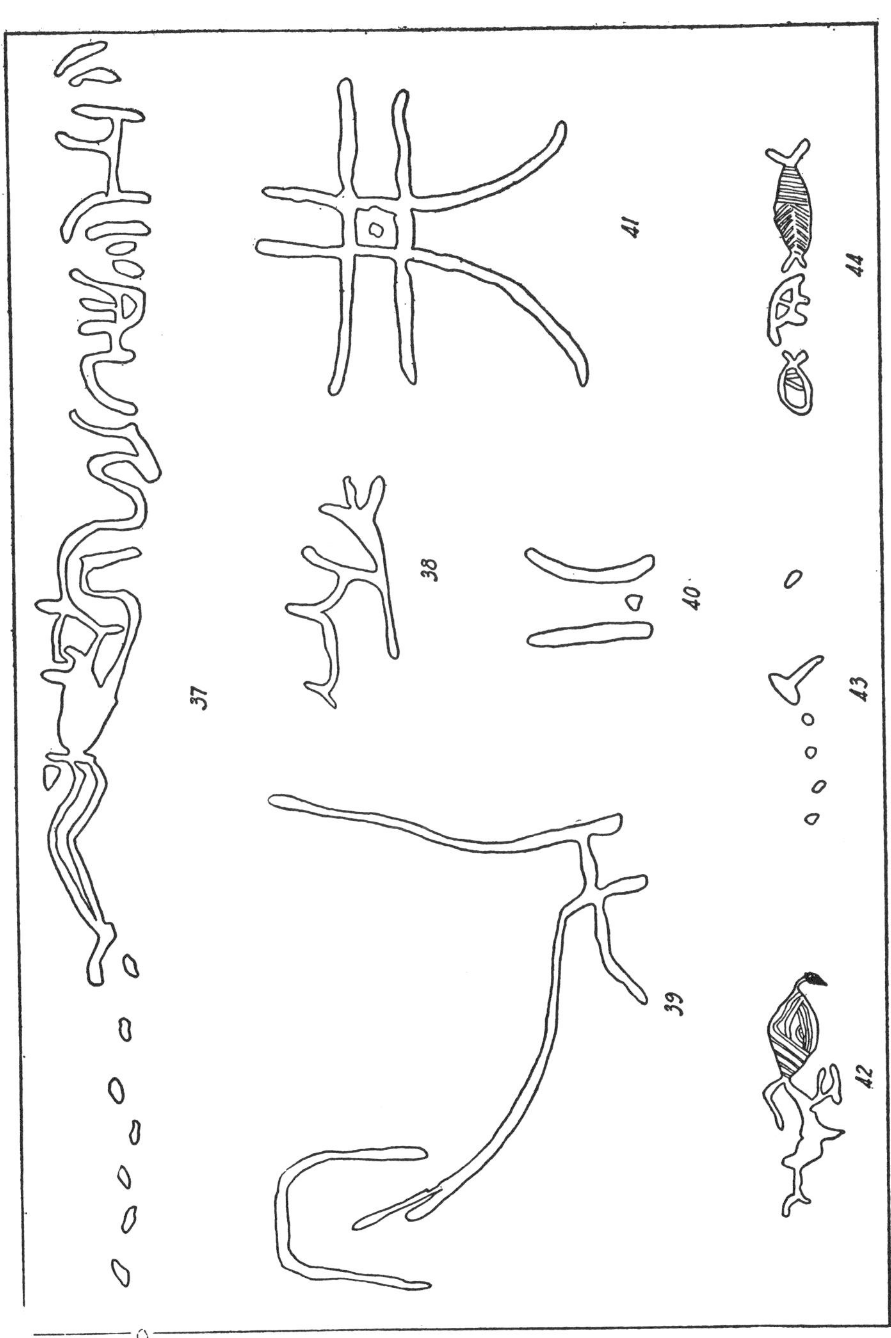
37
38
39
40
41
42
43
44

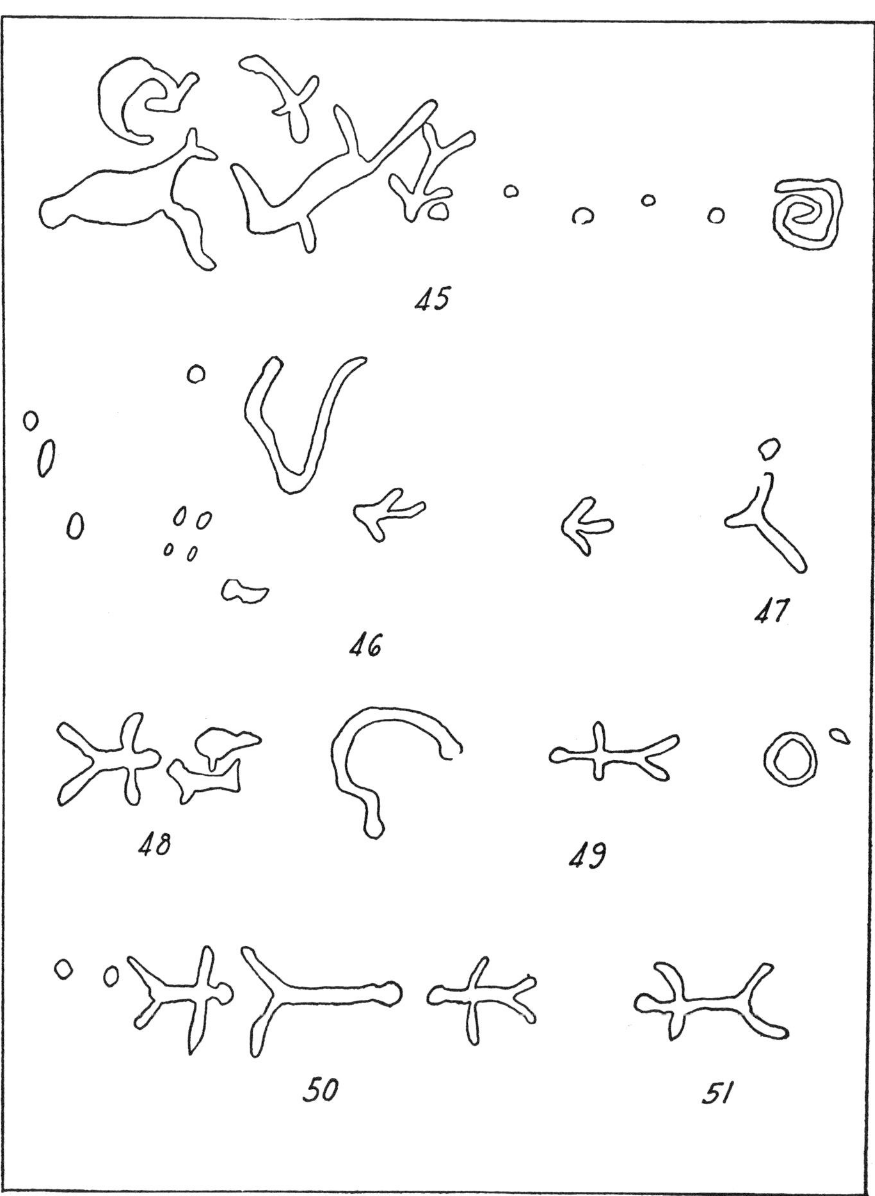
45
46
47
48
49
50
51

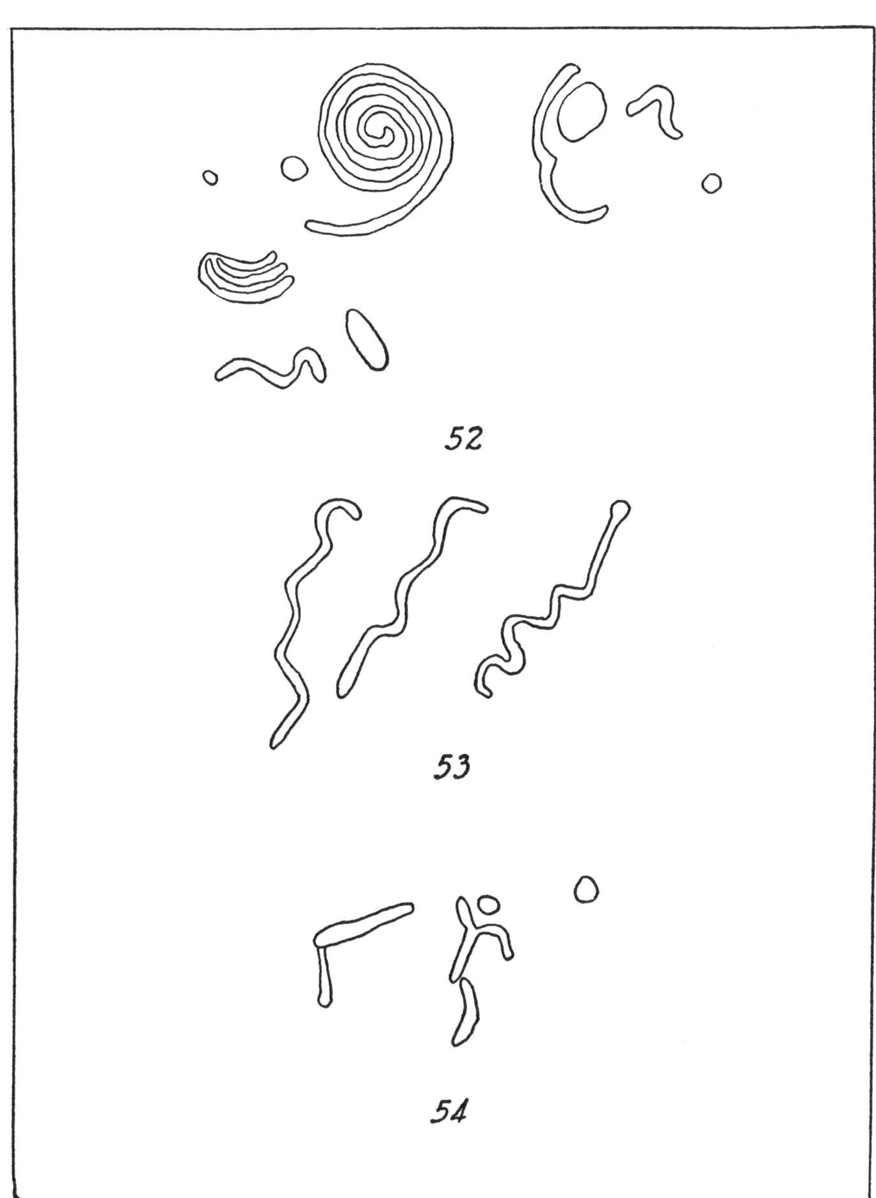
52
53
54

the ideograph referred possessed the power to transport himself or his influence for good or evil through space by means of magic powers.

In figures 26 (upper right) and 37E the Chinese character for a temporary defense, a hill fortress, or a mountain, is represented. The figures in the former group apparently were intended to tell a connected story. Reading from right to left, the interpretation in Chinese reads:

Figure E, mountain or fortress; D, stream; C, forest, wood, grass. The connecting lines in the balance of the figures are indefinite.

Figure 2 is the Chinese symbol for "sun." Figure 10 without the two dots and combined with Figure 9 represents "water" or "lake."

Figure 7 is the numeral "ten" and the separate group on the right of Figure 27 represents the numeral "three."

Figure 31 without the separate group at the top and the perpendicular line underneath represents "of rain" or "heavy rain."

Figures 38, 39 and 40 combined indicates the word "high" or a "prominent point."

Figure 49 indicates "big" while the somewhat similar character figure 51, is "soil."

There are other characters from Walnut Island that apparently have a random resemblance to Chinese writings, but their uncertain interpretation is of no practical scientific value. The comparisons are made here primarily for the purpose of showing what for the present we must consider a somewhat similar development of written characters in parts of the world quite remote from each other. We have no proof that the figures from Walnut Island had the same meaning to the people who made them as similar ones have to the Chinese.

In California an effort has been made by Mr. Julian H. Steward to record for comparative purposes the petroglyphs found in that State (3).

In many respects the Owens Valley, California figures resemble those found upon Creswell Rock. These are represented from 45 to 54. The coil-shaped figures in group 45 and 52 are common in various sections where Indian petroglyphs are found. They have been reported from California, Brazil and in other parts of eastern South America (4). That a similar coil design was used among the Indians of eastern Canada is shown in H. I. Smith's book, *Aboriginal Canadian Art*—Ottawa 1923, Bulletin 37, plate LXXXI.

The conception and style of the Creswell writings is more American than Oriental, and with a few exceptions that may be contemporary with the others, these petroglyphs fall into group one.

In the interior of British Columbia, Canada, Smith reports pictographs similar to the fish-like figures in groups 18 and 28 (Smith fig. 21, plate XXXVIII). In this same region more or less conventionalized figures have been found and attempts made to interpret them by local Indians.

On southern Vancouver Island, Canada, in the Salish Indian area, combined petroglyphs showing what appears to be sea monsters have been recorded.

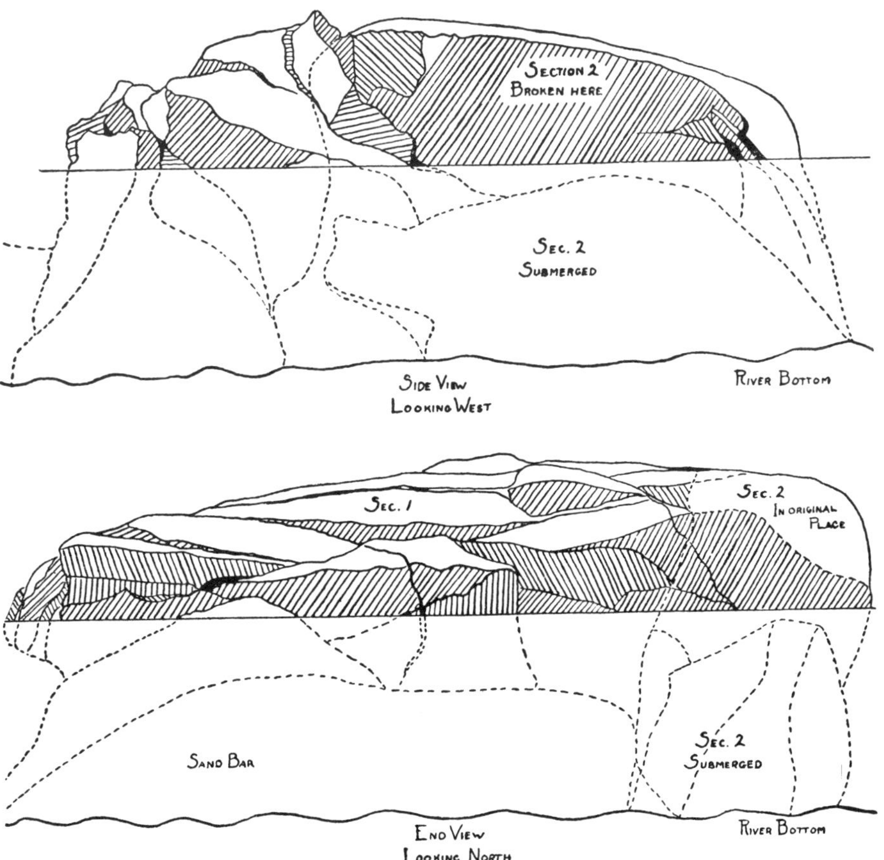

CROSS SECTIONS OF LITTLE INDIAN ROCK

CHAR

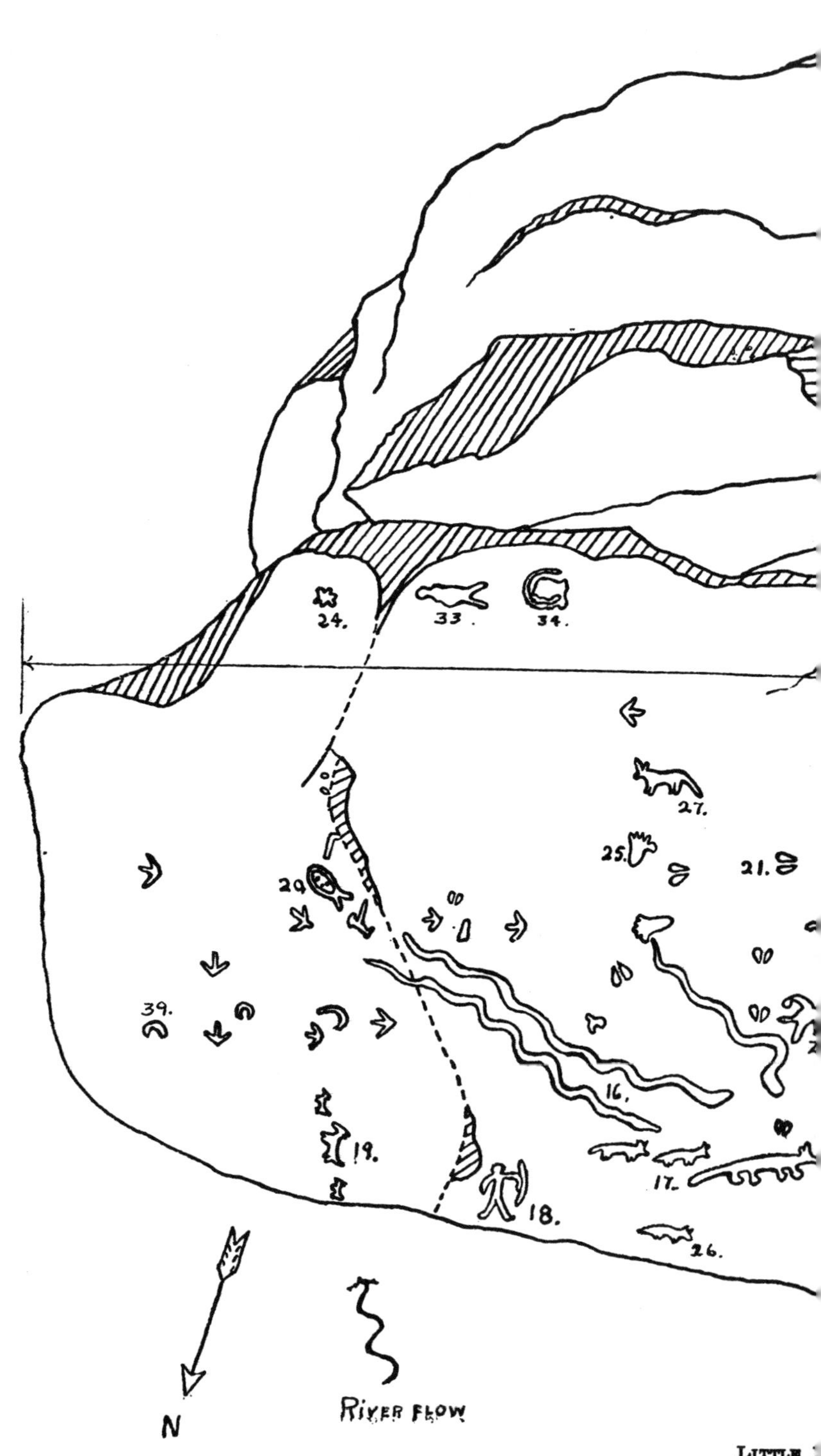

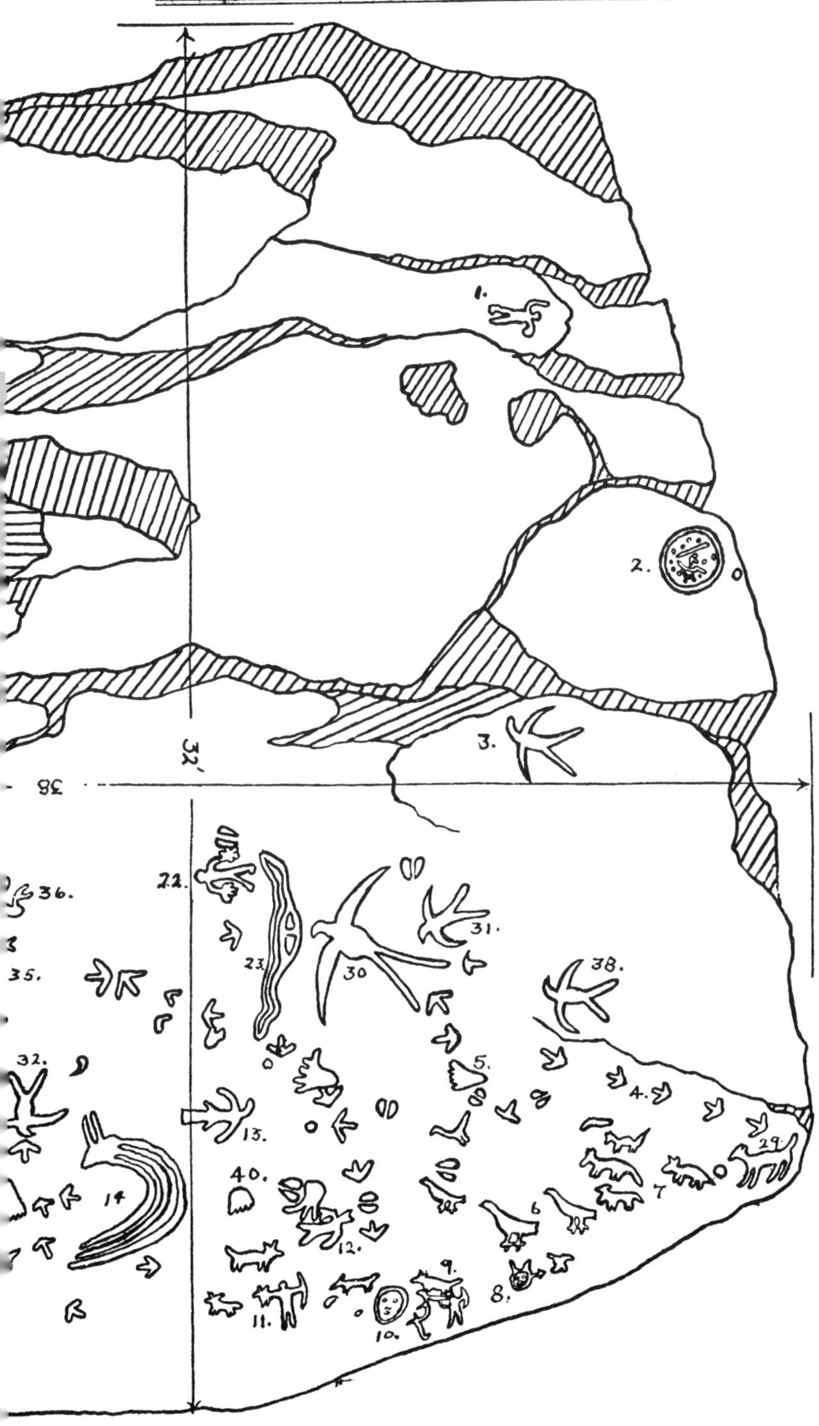

N ROCK

CHART III

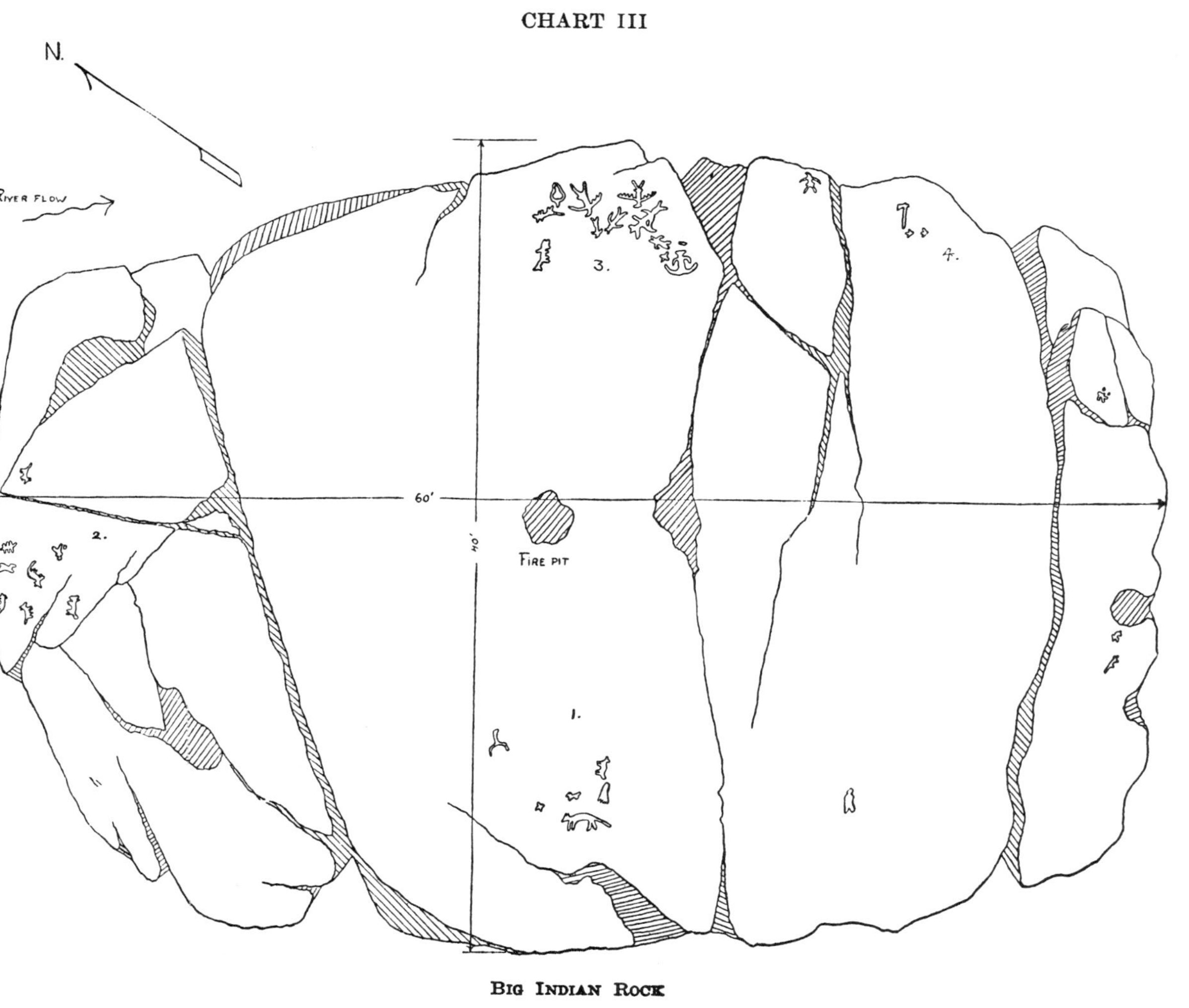

BIG INDIAN ROCK

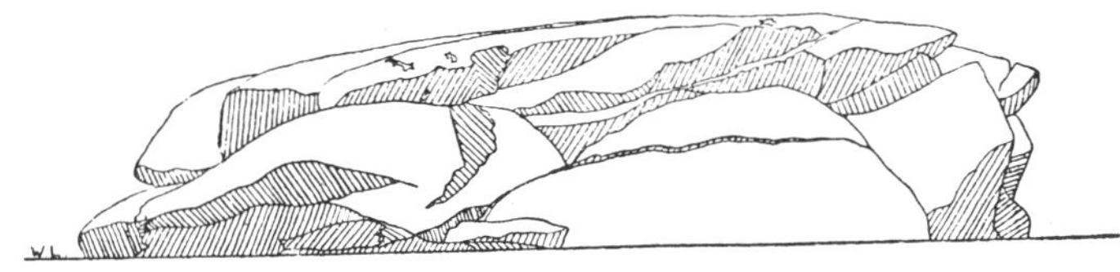

END VIEW
LOOKING NORTH

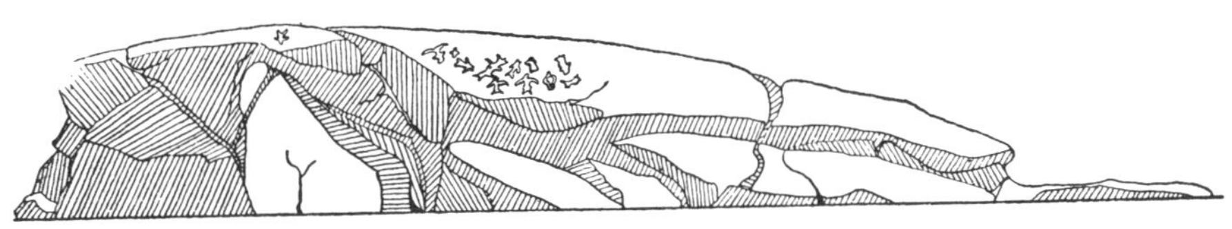

SIDE VIEW
LOOKING WEST

CROSS SECTIONS OF BIG INDIAN ROCK

We cannot close this chapter without some reference to the signatures of the historical Iroquoian and Algonkian chiefs. We find their marks on many of the original land deeds and several of them are conventionalized. An excellent group of these marks is shown in a recent publication of the Gloucester County, New Jersey, Historical Society. Many of these signatures are attempts upon the part of the clerk to portray the totem, clan, or tribal marks of the individual chiefs.

Some of the treaties made by Sir William Johnson with the Iroquois show conventionalized figures for the signatures of several noted chiefs (plate XIII). Numerous examples of these signatures can be found in the archives of the State and in the Historical Society of Pennsylvania.

PLATE XIII

Given under my Hand at Johnson Hall, the third Day of April 1764

Tagaanadie — Sayenqueraghta
Haanijes — Wanughsissae — Wm Johnson
Ohonedagaw — Saganoondie
Aughnawawis — Taanjaqua

SIGNATURES OF IROQUOIS INDIAN CHIEFS ON A TREATY MADE WITH THEM BY SIR WILLIAM JOHNSON

Big and Little Indian Rocks

The petroglyphs on Big and Little Indian Rocks belong in group two and are of zoömorphic character. These figures were first identified as Algonkian by Colonel Garrick Mallery of the Bureau of American Ethnology, Washington, D. C. (6).

Since his identification, the general resemblance of characters in pictographs within certain archaelogically known areas has been sufficiently persistent to suggest the existence of pictorial relationship between various tribes. We agree with Mr. Mallery's identification of the figures because of established nearby contemporary archaelogical evidence, and the fact that they are similar to characters still in use by groups of the same stock.

This type of zoömorphic pictograph, however, is generally independent of language and purely mnemonic. The stage in the development of writing in which ideograms evolve into phonograms usually does not apply to zoömorphic figures, because pictures representing things and thoughts were derived from conventionalized pictures which represented abstract ideas and sounds.

A tribe of the Algonkian Indians made the ideographs upon Big and Little Indian Rocks probably previous to the Susquehannock-Iroquois invasion and occupation of the region which occurred, according to Dr. Arthur C. Parker's tentative chronology, approximately 1000 A. D. Their drawings are as perfect as it was possible for them to make them, and their representations of various animal and human forms are sincere attempts to record and graphically transmit the thoughts selected for pictorial delineation. They were made to fix in the memory the object or idea by visualizing certain analogies between the symbol and the idea attached to it which the mind sees. The skill of the artists varied; hence when atempting the portrayal of certain animals their end was attained chiefly by emphasizing prominent and unmistakable features.

Some authorities think that all pictographs are based upon the sign language (7). Unquestionably gesture lines were used by some groups to convey ideas, but many of them were beyond the skill of an artist to portray on a flat stone surface when equipped only with a stone chisel. He was limited to the presentation of objects in outline. A few of the known gesture signs correspond with ancient rock writings, but in the eastern Algonkian territory, to the best of our knowledge, the Indians did not use the sign language as extensively as other groups farther west.

It is generally believed that the interpretation of many of the ancient forms of Indian writings may be obtained by an understanding of more modern forms, some of which can be interpreted by living men. When this method fails and the identification of culture is conceded, some of the forms can be made intelligible by a thorough knowledge of the linguistic group involved, including their social organization and material culture.

Ample proof exists that the pictographs on Big and Little Indian Rocks bear a striking resemblance to mnemonic figures made and still used by the Ojibway Indians. The similarity was first observed by Doctor Hoffman, and in his *Geographical Distribution of Pictographs on the Susquehanna River,* he says: "Farther up the river, at Safe Harbor, Pennsylvania, is another series of petroglyphs of a more distinctly Algonkian type, resembling in fact, characters found among the birchbark records of living Ojibway Indians." (8).

Mr. Garrick Mallery in referring to the same group says: "This appears to be purely Algonkian and has more resemblance to Ojibway characters than any other petroglyphs yet noted from the Eastern United States." (9).

The limits of this report do not allow us to cover the neglected field of early Algonkian Indian symbolism, a complete study of which would carry us back to ancient horizons of culture. Its progress was arrested by the Iroquoian and white invasion before indirect signs of sound had suspended direct presentment of sight for communication and record.

Contemporary archaeological evidence, where it can be established, is the most valuable means of identifying culture. Near Big and Little Indian Rocks, at Shenk's Ferry, a definite Algonkian culture, probably contemporary with the petroglyphs, has been established. But, outside of the fact that this culture is prehistoric, it is impossible at the present time to place it accurately in a distinct period. An authentic archaeological chronology of Algonkian and Iroquois occupation, together with established criteria, is sadly lacking in Pennsylvania.

There is no direct information to be obtained concerning the interpretation of the Algonkian pictographs at Safe Harbor.

The only way they can be studied is with a collection of known characters such as those used by historic tribes.

We cannot attempt to describe early eastern Algonkian symbolism without some reference to the writings of Constantine Samuel Raffinesque-Schmaltz. To this visionary Philadelphian of the early eighteen hundreds we owe the preservation and first translation of the Walam Olum of the Lenape, or Delaware Indians.

Raffinesque was a prolific writer and dipped into many fields of science. In his later years he became interested in the Indians, and if for no other reason than the preservation of the Walam Olum, we have to take his interpretations of Indian writings seriously. In his *Lenape Annals* he says: "We knew by all the writers who have had friendly intercourse with the tribes of North America, that they did possess, and perhaps keep yet, historical and traditional records of events, by hieroglyphs or symbols, on wood, bark, skins, in stringed wampums, etc.; but none had been published in the original form." (10) (p. 122).

Raffinesque was an erractic writer, but in view of recent studies of Algonkian Indian pictographs, his records are surprisingly accurate. Among the Ojibway, especially in connection with their "Midèwin" or Medicine Lodge records, we still find many of his figures, and their interpretations are similar.

The exact source of the Walam Olum is somewhat doubtful, and it is supposed to follow the history of the Lenape from 1820 far back into the past. The antiquity of the figures, especially the composite ones, is doubtful, although the migration story and the legends may be fairly authentic.

Loskiel, writing about the Delawares in 1794 said:

"But though they are indifferent about the history of former times, and ignorant of the art of reading and writing, yet their ancestors were well aware that they stood in need of something to enable them to convey their ideas to a distant nation, or to preserve the memory of remarkable events at least for a season. To this end they invented something like hieroglyphics, and also strings and belts of wanpon.

"Their hieroglyphics or characteristic figures are more frequently painted upon trees than cut in stone. They are intended either to caution against danger, to mark a place of safety, to direct the wanderer into the right path, to record a remarkable transaction, or to commemorate the deeds and achievements of their celebrated heroes, and are as intelligible to them as a written account is to us." (11).

We believe zoömorphic pictographs were used for a great variety of serious purposes. That they are not scrawls made to occupy idle moments has been definitely proved by a continuation of similar symbols among living groups. Some of them represent mythology and religious practices as portrayed by individuals and members of various secret societies. Others are representations of animals or birds and may indicate success in hunting. Depicted in certain places, they give notice that game could be found in that locality. Many of them relate to mythical beings and deities of imaginary form. Undoubtedly, too, records of important events and visitors were perpetuated in stone.

Among some of the groups using pictographic records, especially the Ojibway and Pueblo Indians, certain determinations are used with figures intended to be supernatural. In our comparative identification of some of the Algonkian records near Safe Harbor we will use the Ojibway designations if indicated.

It is unfortunate that so many of the component parts of the Safe Harbor figures have been destroyed. Frazer bewailed this fact in 1889 and since that time considerably more damage has been done. However, we will do our best to present here the indirect translations that are intelligible according to modern investigators:

Comparative Interpretations of Symbols

Little Indian Rock

Chart 2.

1. Human figure with right arm raised.
Among certain Algonkian groups the raising of the right hand was the sign for peace. The left hand indicated treachery.
Supplication to the Great Spirit.
Indicates a beggar.
Indicates a hermit.

2. A concentric circle within which several indeterminate figures are depicted.
Double lines indicate supernatural.
An enclosure.
Symbolical of a great feast.
A feast dish.
A hole in the ground or a cache.

3. Thunderbird.

30. Thunderbird. A symbol still used among living groups of Algonkians.

31. Thunderbird. Flying gods were always considered friendly ones.

32A. Thunderbird. Crawling or swimming gods brought evil.
Thunder and lightning were supposed to be produced by birds of enormous size. These beings produced thunder by flapping their wings and lightning by opening and closing their eyes. The downpour which generally accompanies thunder was accounted for by a lake of fresh water the bird carried upon its back and shook out when it flapped its wings. Some Algonkian tribes had only one thunderbird, among others there was a family of them represented in various sizes and colors.

4,35. Turkey tracks.

5,25. Bear tracks.

15. Human tracks.

21. Buffalo, deer, and elk tracks.

40. Otter tracks.

It is impossible to determine whether these ideaographs are supposed to represent the animal as a totem, a track, or a personal name. They do not indicate any particular direction and may be interpreted as symbols of hunting feats. At one time some of them were combined with other figures that have been destroyed.

The bear tracks are indicated by pronounced big toes and a short foot while the human footmark is unquestionable.

6. Turkeys.

These may be totemic, but probably indicate that this bird can be found to the eastward.

Most Algonkian tribes associated themselves with certain animals and the custom still survives among living groups. Among the Lenape there was one powerful group called the Unalâchtigo, meaning "the turkey."

Heckewelder, writing about this group says: "The merits of the Turkey, which gives its name to the second tribe, are that he is stationary, and always remains with or about them. Those of the Turkey tribe paint only one foot of a turkey, and the Wolf tribe sometimes a wolf at large with one leg and foot raised up to serve as a hand," etc. (12) (p. 253).

7. Groups and individual animals of various kinds.

In group 7 we find two long-tailed animals and two short-tailed ones. The upper figure may indicate a fox or a skunk and the one just below either an otter or a panther.

29. Figure 29 is a long-legged, long-tailed animal and may belong with group 7. If it does, the circle below the nose indicates that it has certain magical powers that the other animals do not possess.

17. Groups 17 and 26 undoubtedly represent four panthers or otters facing a short-tailed animal which is either a wolf or a dog.

19. Group 19 has one large, long-nosed, short-tailed animal with a similar but smaller figure in front of it, and another in back. Among the Bungi Indians this figure is used to indicate the brown bear who leveled the earth at the beginning of life so that it could be lived upon by the Indians, and it also represents the earth mother who taught the Indians how to use roots for food and medicine.

8. Figure 8 is a human face upon which two ears or horns are depicted. This shows superiority in rank, as a chief or a shaman who is the meditator between the world of spirits and the world of men. This particular figure is probably a shaman as it has what appears to be an arrow or spear projecting from the left side of the face indicative of supernatural power.

20. Number 20 is also that of a human head with horns and shows superiority in rank, as a chief. The double line around the head indicates supernatural power.

12. Figure 12 represents the form of a horned being and could be interpreted in several ways. The large object near the right hand might show that this chief or shaman was well supplied with wordly goods, or it might mean that he kept his medicine in a large bag. The large short-tailed, long-eared animal, together with buffalo, turkey, and bear tracks closely associated with this figure, however, suggests that whoever it is, is supposed to be a mighty hunter.

9. This is a composite group partly obliterated, destroying the possible meaning of the whole. The animal, probably a wolf, standing upon the head of a human with a bow in his left hand might represent a proper name. It may also show that this hunter, identified by the destroyed part of the figure, is a member of the Wolf Clan.

10. The head of a human who has supernatural power, the latter being indicated by the double line around the head and the circle a short distance to the right of the face.

11. A group consisting of a human figure with a bow in its left hand and half the body of a wolf as its right hand. At the left a dog is depicted and at its right a wolf with its head turned to face the figure.

The interpretation of this group according to Beatty and Tannah, Bungi Indians (Prarie Ojibway) and members of the fourth degree of the Midewin, is as follows:

"This man belongs to the Wolf Clan; he can change

PLATE IX

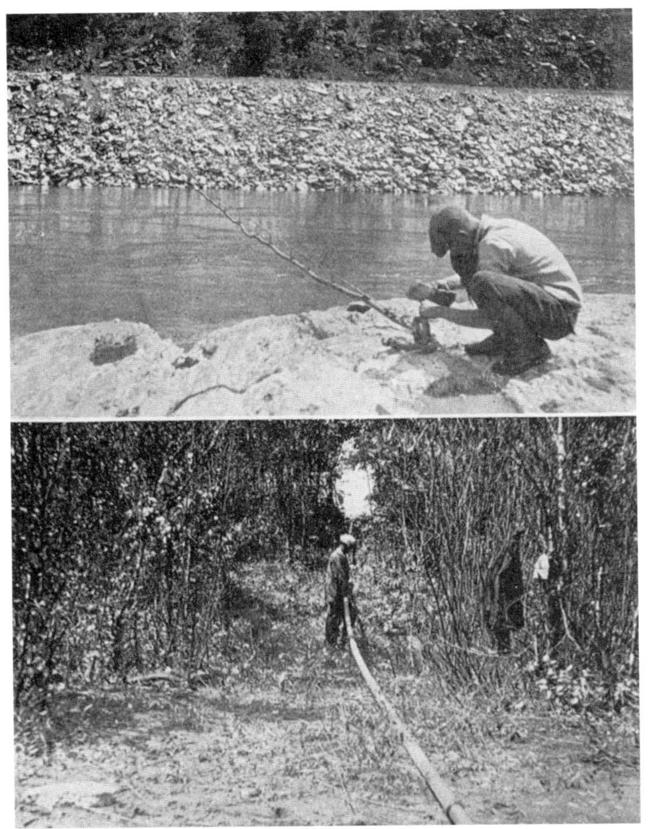

A—Stretching a Cable From the Shore to Walnut Island
B—Pipe Line Running Across the Island

PLATE X

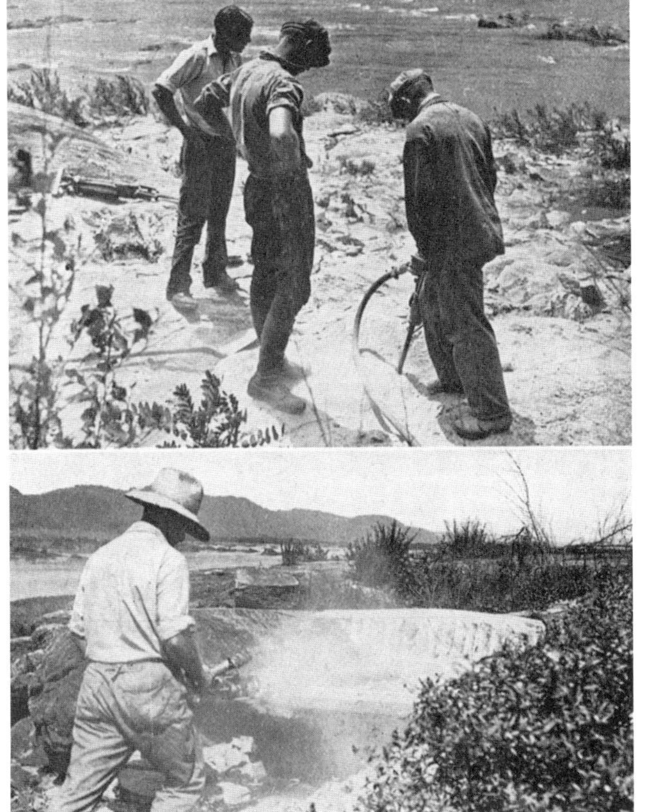

A—The First Hole Drilled After the Air Line Was Completed
B—Drilling Holes on a Plane With the Surface to Remove Pictographs

PLATE XI

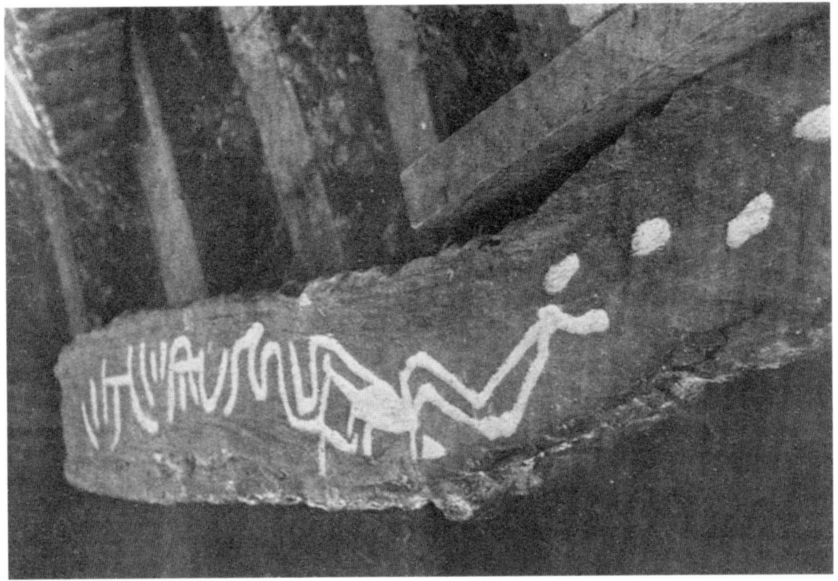

An Unusually Interesting Petroglyph From Walnut Island

PLATE XII

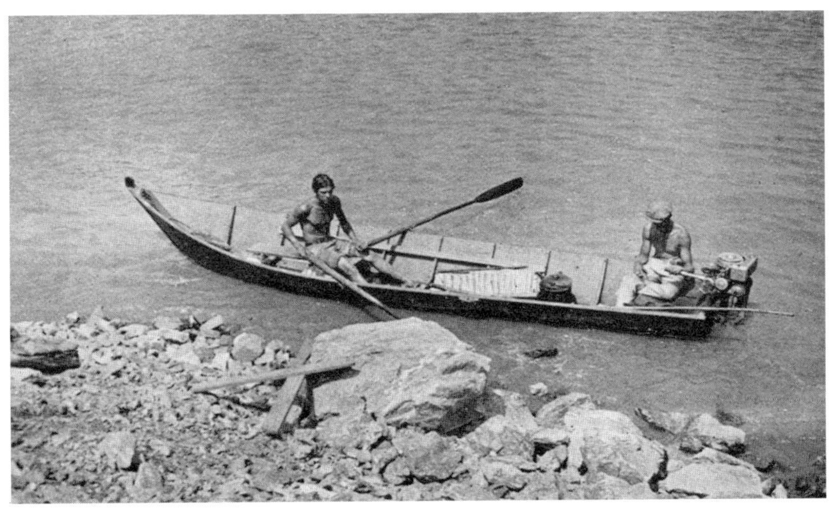

Landing the Rocks at Safe Harbor After Running the Rapids

himself into a wolf as shown by part of his body being indicated as the forepart of a wolf. He is a mighty hunter and is protected at all times by the great ruler of the wolves shown at his left."

The bow shows that the man was a hunter and part of his body being that of a wolf means he could change himself into that animal. The wolf with its head turned toward the hunter indicates that he was successful in killing this animal. The small circle in front of the nose of the wolf on his left shows that this particular animal with supernatural powers, was probably his protector or totem.

13. A thunderbird or eagle upon a pedestal. This might commemorate some unusual occurrence. What appears to be a pedestal may be intended to represent a tail. The Ojibway occasionally depict a thunderbird or an eagle perched upon a medicine pole near a shaman's structure. This is supposed to show that the shaman professes to have the power of flight equal to that of the bird.

14. This character is represented as a bird by Professor Porter whose drawings were made from the plaster molds in the Linnaean Society at Lancaster, Pennsylvania. A close examination of the figure itself revealed several additional concentric lines not shown in the Porter sketch. The part shown as the rounded head of a bird is pointed, the beaks are much wider apart than represented and the whole conception is changed. Instead of a bird, a horned object is indicated, and it may be one of the powerful underground spirits believed in by the early Algonkians. These beings were supposed to have an evil influence and usually are depicted with a round head and horns. If a single line is drawn across the figure, the monster comes out of the earth. A double line means water. The water beings did not have the power for evil that the ground monsters were supposed to have.

16. Indicating the banks of a river, or snakes.

The snake appears in Algonkian mythology as an evil spirit. It symbolizes stealth, but when a feather is attached it represents bravery.

A powerful evil spirit that was supposed to live under the water is often represented with the body of a snake.

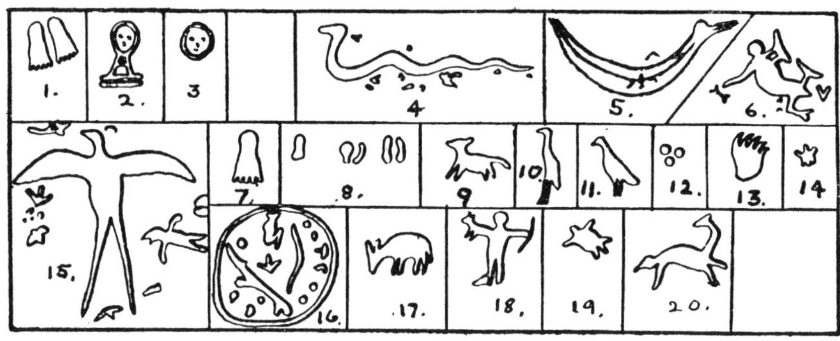

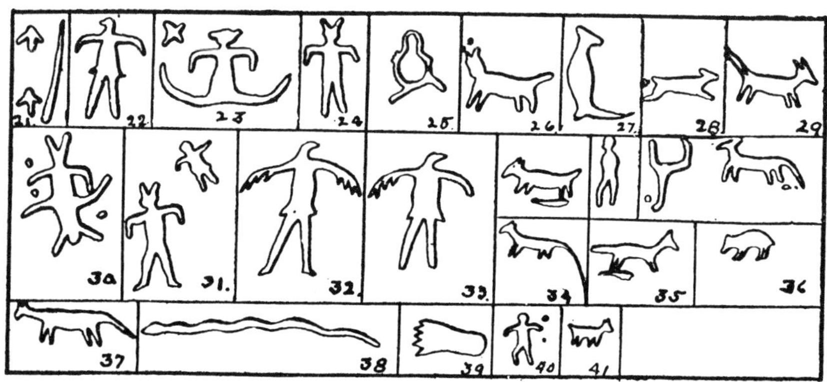

DRAWINGS OF LITTLE INDIAN PETROGLYPHS MADE BY PROFESSOR PORTER

If a figure of some animal or human was depicted between the lines, it would indicate that the person or animal was traveling along the river.

18. A hunter with a bow in his left hand.

22. Human figure with unusually large hands.
Human figure carrying two packages.

23. A snake within an enclosure.
A turtle that has conquered a snake.

24,34.
32B,36.
39. } Indeterminate and partially destroyed figures.
28.
33.

BIG INDIAN ROCK

Chart 3

The figures upon this rock probably are contemporaneous with those upon Little Indian. Many of the symbols were completely destroyed by vandals, others had eroded to such an extent that it was impossible to trace the complete figure.

There is one doubtful figure of an axe in group 4, and dozens of spurious figures were left out of the drawing. The large figure of the "dove of peace" destroyed innumerable symbols between groups 2 and 3.

The spot marked "fire pit" on the drawing showed that many fires had been made there. Whether they were ceremonial fires of the Indians or built by white shad fishermen is questionable.

Conclusions

In this brief report it would have been a simple matter to write the known facts about the petroglyphs in the Safe Harbor area, to show photographs and charts, and leave them for future students to present possible interpretations. We realize that we are treading upon dangerous ground when we compare Susquehanna River records with Oriental writings. Sketches and photographs of the petroglyphs have been submitted to various authorities; they admit the resemblance but refuse to commit themselves. Here we run into the cold light of pure science which demands positive proof and a statement of facts.

The lack of evidence contemporary with most petroglyphs has led many serious students into other fields and away from these records. As a result, theories without the slightest bit of evidence have been advanced as facts and topers of the mysterious have delighted in many new infusions of imagination.

In this report all the comparative interpretations are indirect, as there is no positive proof that the symbols had the same meaning to their makers hundreds of years ago as they have to surviving groups of the same stock, or to people who lived thousands of miles away.

There is always some doubt attached to historical information obtained by a study of pictographs. It is almost impossible to establish direct contemporary evidence and because of this only indefinite conclusions can be reached. We know the figures were important to their authors who were recording history to the best of their ability. Undoubtedly, objects of interest to them were made just to pass time, but, regardless of this, the character of the figures tells us something about the mental ability of those who made them. The others tell the story of their art, customs and religion.

It is admitted by all eastern archaeologists that the earliest known Indians in this area were Algonkians. The Iroquoian groups found here by the first white men were invaders. Mentally, the Algonkians were the inferior group, and we believe they were not capable of developing the complex conventionalized figures found upon Walnut Island. Archaeological evidence has given us the material culture of the invaders, and their social organization is known.

To the best of our knowledge the Walnut Island writing is

PLATE XVI

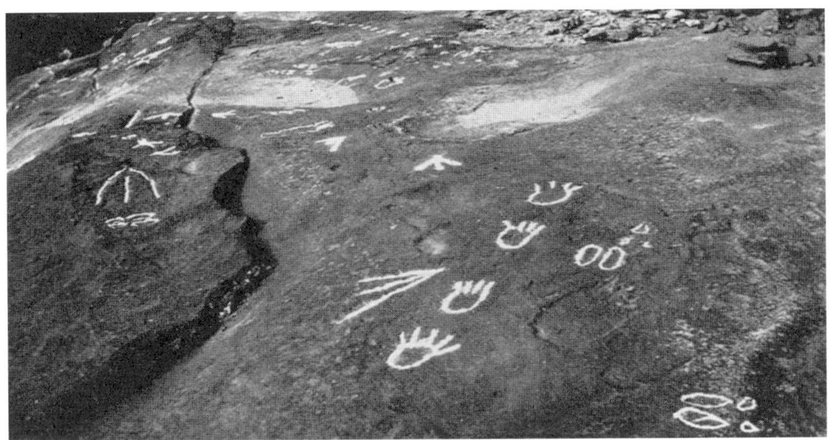

Petroglyphs on the Monongahela River Near New Geneva

PLATE XVII

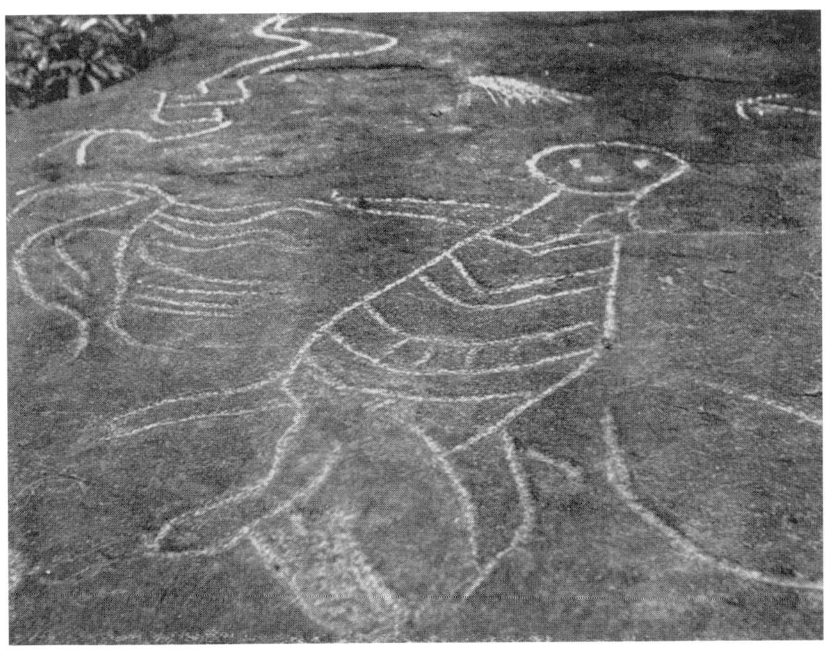

A Figure Suggestive of the Spirit Otter or Underworld Panther of the Lenape Indians

PLATE XVIII

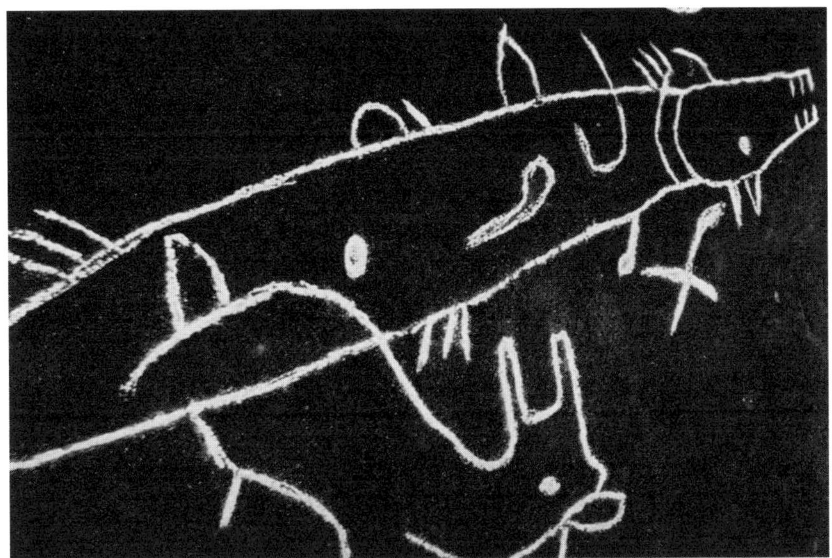

PETROGLYPHS AT SUGAR GROVE

PLATE XIX

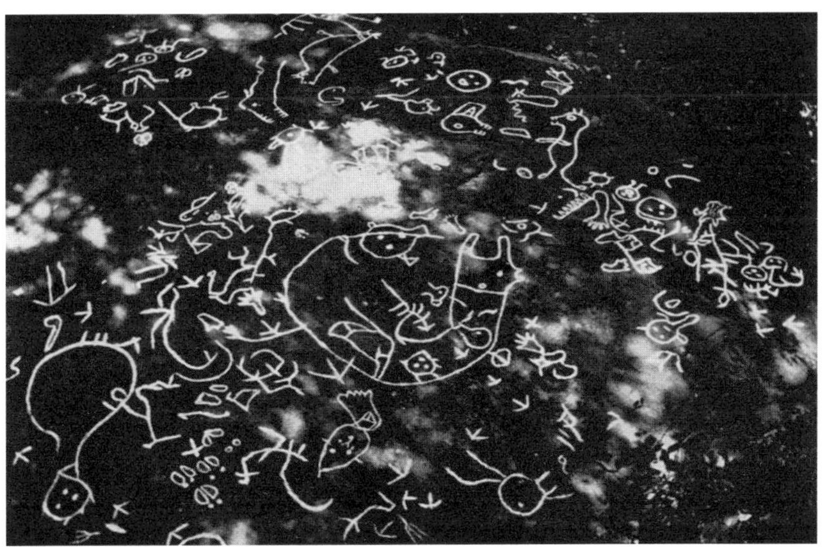

PETROGLYPHS AT SUGAR GROVE, GREENE COUNTY, PENNSYLVANIA

neither Algonkian nor Iroquoian. A two-year archaeological search on the islands, as well as upon the mainland, has failed to reveal human occupation contemporary with the conventionalized writings. An archaeological site on the mainland near Big and Little Indian Rocks showed possible evidence of an Algonkian occupation contemporary with the figures found at this point. A thin disturbed layer of prehistoric Algonkian culture was discovered in the earth on many of the islands in the area as well as on the mainland. On Walnut Island this culture layer was separated from some of the conventionalized figures by a covering of about eight feet of hard packed soil. This is apparent geological evidence that a considerable time had passed between the periods when the two groups of people lived in the Susquehanna Valley.

This discovery presents an unusual situation, contrary to the usual progress of human life. It indicates that a people lived and passed away in Pennsylvania previous to its occupation by known Indians. The early group had reached a state of civilization far in advance of their successors, and the highly conventionalized petroglyphs may represent the only intellectual remains of these inhabitants of the lower Susquehanna Valley. Who these people were and to what era they belong, we do not know. Search for local archaeological evidence contemporary with the figures failed to establish any definite criteria, and we have been forced to believe that this evidence has been washed away or is so scattered, or so deep in the earth, that it may be impossible to establish it with any degree of scientific accuracy.

All available and known American records have been investigated in our comparative study. This has led us far afield and along paths of fact and fancy dangerous to an anthropologist. About the antiquity and culture of early man on the American Continents much is still to be learned, and occasional bits of evidence of an advanced culture are brought to light in North America. We think superior groups migrated onto this continent from the northwest. We know civilized Indians occupied vast areas in Central and South America. The great mounds in Western Pennsylvania, Ohio and in other states, never have been thoroughly explained. Archaeological research is still in its infancy in the United States and we hope that facts about human occupation, still to be recorded, will shed more light upon the conventionalized Safe Harbor records.

In various parts of the territory formerly occupied by the Algonkians many linear-zoömorphic records, similar to those found upon Big and Little Indian Rocks, have been found. The closest comparative interpretative study can be made with those still in use by the Chippewa and Bungi Indians of Canada.

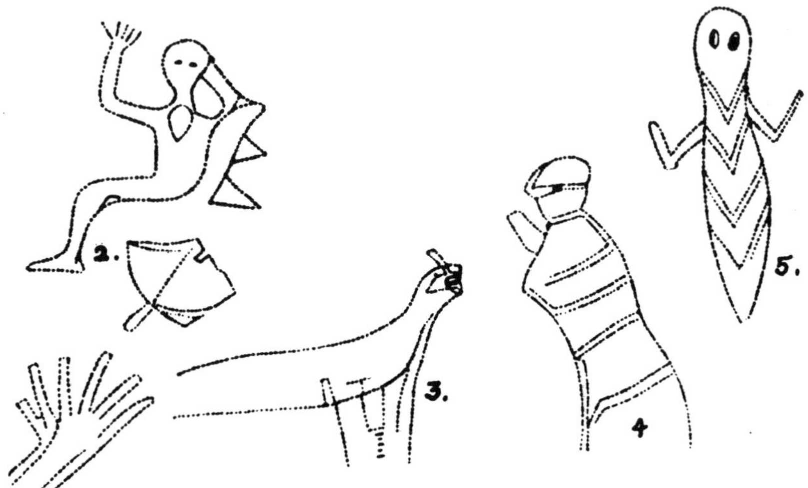

A GROUP OF PICTOGRAPHS ON THE FRANCIS FARM IN FAYETTE COUNTY, PA.

Ample evidence can be produced from historical writings and documents to show that the Leni-Lenape, or Delaware, had a knowledge of mnemonic records. That they were still using them in the late seventeen and early eighteen hundreds is shown by the following account of the Reverend John Heckewelder:

"The Indians do not possess our art of writing, they have no alphabets, or any mode of representing to the eye the sounds of words spoken, yet they have certain hieroglyphics, by which they describe facts in so plain a manner, that those who are conversant with these marks can understand them with the greatest ease, as easily indeed, as we can understand a piece of writing. All Indian nations can do this, although they have not the same marks; yet I have seen the Delawares read with ease the drawings of the Chippeways, Mingoes, Shawanos, and Wyandots, on similar subjects." (12) (p. 130).

It is generally believed that the Lenape migrated across Pennsylvania from west to east in prehistoric times. Within the historic period they migrated westward. The Unami, one of the three principal divisions of the Lenape, at one time occupied a considerable portion of the territory between the Delaware and Susquehanna Rivers from the Lehigh south to Chesapeake Bay. Most of the surviving Lenape now living in Oklahoma seem to be of Unami extraction, according to Mr. M. R. Harrington (13).

In all probability the figures upon Big and Little Indian Rocks were made by the Unami or other Lenape groups that lived in the region before the Iroquois invasion.

Figure 23 on chart 2 may represent a turtle. This testudinate reptile was the totem of the Unami. The Walum Olum indicates that they had considerable difficulty with a group they called the "snakes" on their migration eastward. Without using our imagination too far, figure 23 might indicate the subjection or absorption of the "snake people."

Later the Iroquois groups in what is now New York State were called "snakes" by the Lenape. This might show that anything that brought evil to them was given this appellation. It is also possible that the Lenape on their way eastward may have encountered a northeastward bound group of migrating Iroquois and the name survived until historic times. Various theories could be advanced, but, like the absolute authenticity of the Walum Olum, they would lack accurate scientific proof.

The nearest comparative petroglyphs to those found on Big and Little Indian Rocks are in Ohio. They are known as the Barnesville Track Rocks and the Newark Track Rock. These were recorded by Dr. J. Walton and Dr. J. Salsbury in 1869 and 1871, and are described and illustrated in the first number of the *American Anthropological Journal* in 1872. (15) (p. 89).

Most of the figures at these two points in Ohio, are similar to those on Little Indian Rock. The treatment of the characters is almost identical and the conception is probably the same. The bear tracks have the outside toe distorted and there are innumerable animal and bird tracks, the latter presumably of a turkey. The identification symbol of the Unalâchtigo Lenape was the track of the turkey, as previously cited.

The "thunderbird" is missing upon the Ohio rocks but is found in various forms on the Susquehanna. If the Pennsylvania petroglyphs were made by the same migrating groups of Algonkian Indians, this symbol was conceived on the road be-

PLATE XIV

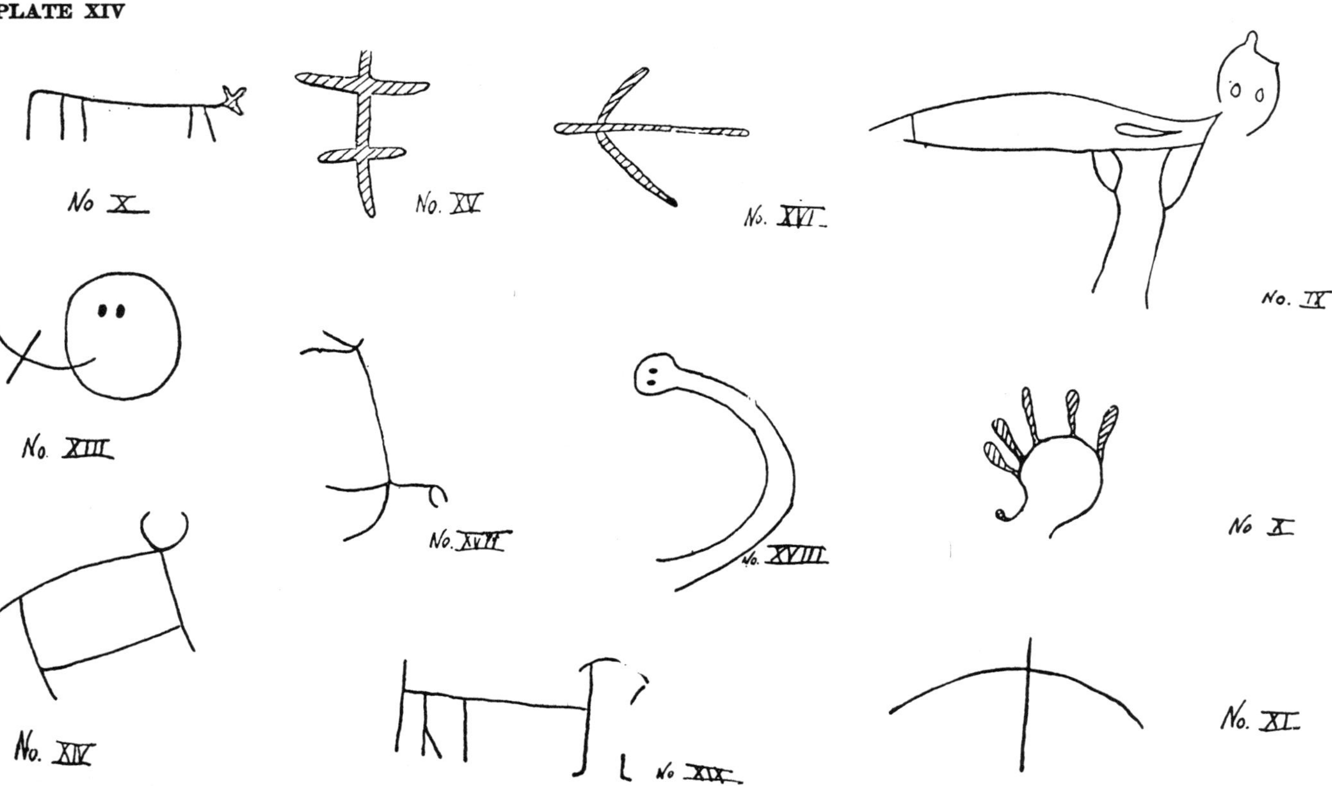

FIGURES APPEARING ON "INDIAN GOD ROCK" IN THE ALLEGHENY RIVER BELOW FRANKLIN

PLATE XV

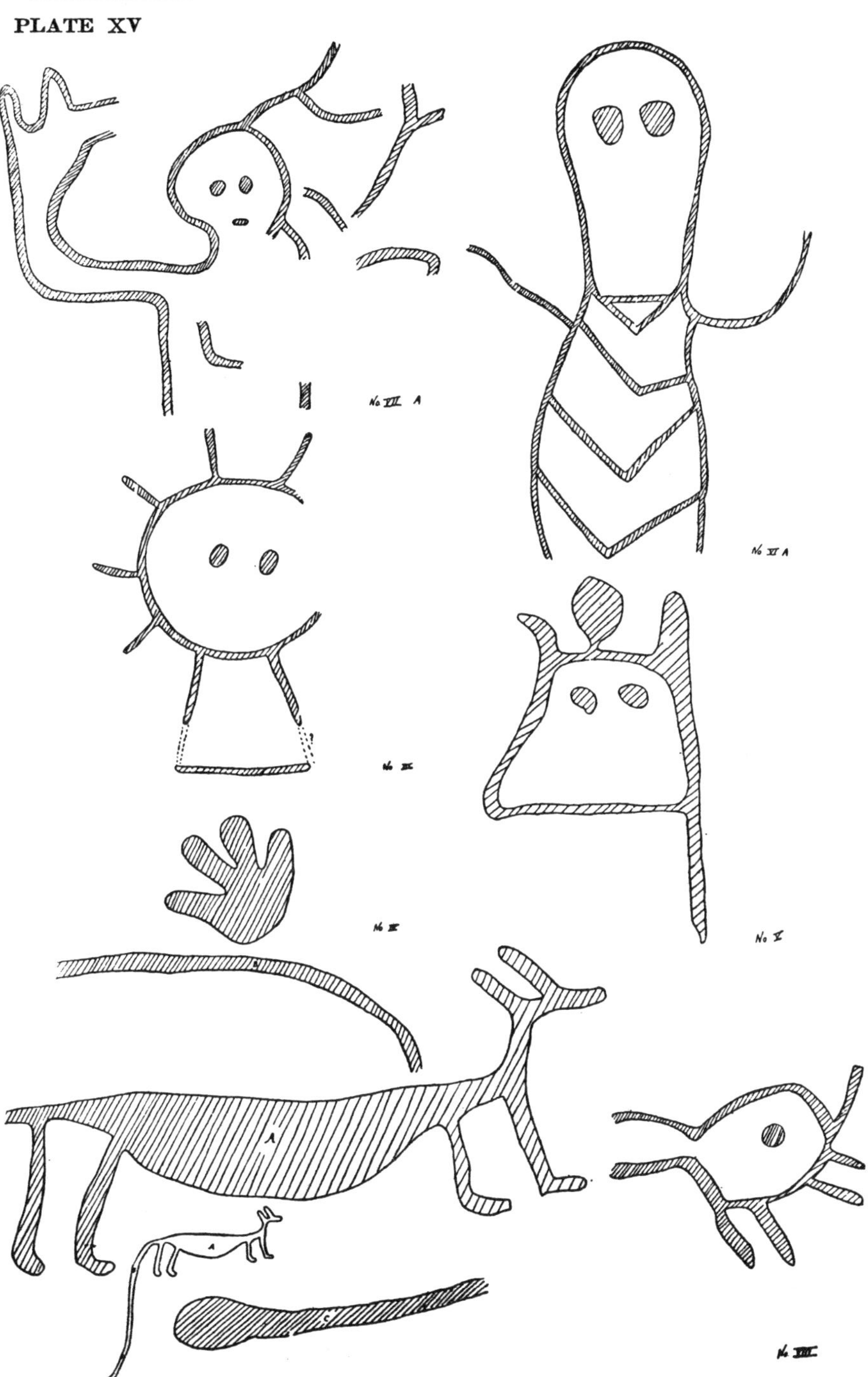

PETROGLYPHS ON INDIAN GOD ROCK

tween the two points, indicating greater antiquity to those in the west and supporting the eastward migration belief.

In the western part of Pennsylvania on the Ohio, Allegheny and Monongahela watersheds, many petroglyphs have been found. These are all of Algonkian type, and perhaps the outstanding group is upon what is known as "Indian God Rock" on the Allegheny River below Franklin. Tracings of this group were made by Mr. Clifford M. Lewis, of Cambridge Springs, Pennsylvania, in 1932 (plates XIV, XV). This rock was visited also in 1886 by Dr. Hoffman who made sketches of the figures. An interesting comparison can be made between his work (Figure 74) and that of Mr. Lewis, who traced the figures directly off the rock and reduced them to scale. These petroglyphs probably are of a later period than those upon Little Indian, as their makers were starting to conventionalize as shown in figures X, XIV, XVII, etc. (plates XIV, XV). Figure XVI may represent the "thunderbird" and XVIII is probably an underground monster as shown in the Walum Olum (I:14-21—II:2-3-36). These symbols can be compared more closely to modern Chippewa characters than those at Safe Harbor. Figures X and III are shamanistic, and, together with symbols similar to XV-A, are used in Midewin ceremonies.

In 1886 Dr. Hoffman said: "The face of the boulder bearing the original petroglyphs has been much disfigured by visitors who, endeavoring to display their skill by pecking upon the surface names, dates, and other designs, have so injured it that it is difficult to trace the original characters."

Mr. Lewis fifty-six years later stated: "The job of tracing out the inscriptions is made extremely hard by the fact that the rock is practically covered with the names and initials of white men."

Petroglyphs of Algonkian type have been found along the Monongahela River about fifty miles south of Pittsburgh and near the town of New Geneva. These were first reported by Mr. J. S. Wall, of Monongahela City in 1882. In 1932, Mr. George Fisher, of Finleyville, photographed these records and reported them as eroding rapidly. (plate XVI). Mr. Fisher also photographed a number of the unusually interesting petroglyphs at Sugar Grove in Greene County (plates XVIII, XIX). This latter group resembles the figures upon "Indian God Rock" more than the simpler forms at New Geneva.

In Fayette County, between Layton and Perryopolis, on what is known as the Francis Farm, a group of pictographs of Algonkian type has been found. These were partially defaced by visitors but are now being protected by the owners of the property. The most prominent figure in this group is the banded monster with the spread legs and a tail (plate XVII). This is strongly suggestive of the spirit otter or underworld panther of the Lenape. These spiritual animals have always played an important part in Lenape ceremonial life as well as in that of the Chippewa.

Innumerable pictographs have disappeared in Pennsylvania within the memory of men still living. Some of them have eroded away and others have been destroyed by thoughtless individuals and industrial expansion. While these records may never play an important part in our history, and men of science frown on interpretation without contemporary evidence, we believe they should be preserved. They represent a chapter of our unknown past, and although many of them may never be deciphered accurately, they are the only intellectual remains of the graphic art of very ancient human life in Pennsylvania.

Notes and Bibliography

1. CADZOW, DONALD A.
Indian Notes, Vol. 3, No. 2.
Heye Foundation, New York—1926.

2. ANNUAL REPORT OF THE BUREAU OF ETHNOLOGY
1888-1889 (p. 107).

3. STEWARD, JULIAN H.
Petroglyphs of California and Adjoining States.
Berkley, California—1929.

4. MALLERY, G.
Picture Writing of the American Indians.
Report of Bureau of American Ethnology—1888-1889.

5. STEWART, F. H.
Indians of Southern New Jersey.
Woodbury—1932 (pp. 58-59).

6. MALLERY, GARRICK
Pictographs of the North American Indians.
Fourth Report of Bureau of American Ethnology—1882-1883 (p. 227).

7. BRINTON, D. G.
The Lenape and Their Legends.
Philadelphia—1885.

8. HOFFMAN, W. J.
The Beginnings of Writing.
New York—1895 (p. 10).

9. SHEAFER, P. W.
Historical Map of Pennsylvania.
Philadelphia—1875.

10. RAFFINESQUE, C. S.
The American Nations.
Philadelphia—1836 (p. 122).

11. LOSKIEL, G. H.
History of the Mission of the United Brethren Among the Indians of North America.
London—1794.

12. HECKEWELDER, THE REVEREND JOHN
The Indian Nations.
Philadelphia—1876 (p. 253).

13. HARRINGTON, M. R.
Religion and Ceremonies of the Lenape.
New York—1921.

14. WRIGHT, WILLIAM
The Empire of the Hittites.
New York—1884 (p. 170).

15. FINAL REPORT—Ohio State Board of Centennial Managers.
Columbus—1877.

---

16. AMERICAN ANTIQUARIAN, Vol. 8, No. 3, May—1886.
Human Faces in Aboriginal Art.

17. AMERICAN INDIAN SERIES
H. R. Mallinson and Company, Inc., New York—1928.

18. ANIMAL FIGURES IN AMERICAN ART
American Antiquarian, Vol. 8, No. 1, January—1886 (pp. 1-48).

19. ARMSTRONG, P. A.
The Piasa, or, the Devil Among the Indians (pp. 1-48).

20. BASSER, H. TH.
Geschichte des Kunstgewerbes. Band II, Verlag. Ernst Wasmuth Ag., Berlin.

21. BOAS, FRANZ
Primitive Art. Oslo, Norway—1927.
Reprint: Instituttet for Sammenlignende Kulturforskning, Serie B, Skrifter, VIII—1927.

22. BRUFF, J. G.
Indian Engravings on the Face of Rocks Along Green River Valley in the Sierra Nevada Range of Mountains.
Washington—1873.
Excerpt: Smithsonian Report for 1872 (pp. 409-412).

23. BUSHNELL, DAVID I., JR.
An Early Account of Dighton Rock.
The New Era Printing Company—1908, Lancaster, Pa.
Reprint: American Anthropologist, n.s., Vol. 10, No. 2. April-June (pp. 251-254).
Petroglyphs Representing the Imprint of the Human Foot.
Excerpt: American Anthropologist, n.s. 15, 1913 (pp. 8-15) pht.

24. CLODD, EDWARD
The Story of the Alphabet.
Appleton—1928.

25. COLLINS, HENRY B., JR.

Prehistoric Art of the Alaskan Eskimo.
In: Smithsonian Miscellaneous Collections, Vol. 81, No. 14, November 1929. Publication 3023 (pp. 1-52).

26. COPWAY

The Traditional History and Characteristic Sketches of the Ojibway Nation.
London—1850.

27. DAVIS, ROBERT H.

Nevada Footprints.
Excerpt: California Magazine, September, 1893 (pp. 598-605).

28. DELAHARRE, EDMUND BURKE

Dighton Rock, A Study of the Written Rocks of New England.
Neale.

29. EMERSON, ELLEN RUSSELL

Repetition in Picture Writing.
Meridon, Illinois—1889.
Excerpt: Bound with Wright, G. F., Idaho First. q. v.

30. ENGERRAND, G.

Nouveaux petroglyphs de la Basse-Californie. Paris, Ecole d' Anthropologie.

31. ENGLISH, TOM

The Piasa Petroglyph: The Devourer from the Bluffs.
In: Art and Archaeology, Vol. 14, No. 3, September-1922.

32. FASCINATING SYMBOLISM OF BEADS.

In: Gas Logic, Vol. 43, No. 2, New York, August—1927.

33. FREE, E. E.

Mysterious String Figures Still Made by Indians. New York, n. p., 1927.
In: The Week's Science, November 21, 1927 (mimeographed).

34. GARDNER, G. A.

Rock-paintings of North West Cordoba (Argentina).
Clarendon Press, Oxford.

35. GREEN, EDWARD

Ancient Rock Inscriptions in Johnson County, Arkansas.

36. HARRINGTON, M. R.
Form and Color in American Indian Pottery North of Mexico.
Reprint: Journal of the American Ceramic Society.
Vol. 10, No. 7, July 1927.

37. HATT, GUDMUND
Arktiske Skinddragter I Eurasien Og Amerika: en ethnogrfisk studie.
Copenhagen, J. H. Schultz Forlagsboghandel—1914.

38. HENSHAW, W. H.
Animal Carvings—1886.
Excerpt: American Antiquarian, March—1886.
(pp. 102-108)

39. HODGE, ZAHRAH PREBLE
Copies of Rock-Paintings in a Cave Near Exeter, Tulare County, California.

40. HOFFMAN, WALTER JAMES
The Graphic Art of the Eskimo.
Washington—1897.
Reprint: United States National Museum Report for 1895.

41. HOLDEN, EDWARD SINGLETON (1846-1914)
Studies in Central American Picture Writing.
In: United States Bureau of American Ethnology. First Annual Report—1879-1880.
Washington—1881 (pp. 205-245)

42. HOLMES, WILLIAM H.
On the Evolution of Ornament: An American Lesson.
Reprint: American Anthropologist, April 1890.

43. JOMARD
Seconde note sur une pierre gravee dans un ancien tumulus Americain...Lee a L'Academie des Inscriptions et Belles-Lettres, le 7 november, 1845.

44. KEANE, A. H.
Native American Culture—1902.
Excerpt: International Monthly, Vol. 5, No. 3, March (pp. 338-357).

45. KINGSBOROUGH
Vol. II, Codex Viennensis.

46. KRICKEBERG, WALTER
Das Kunstgebwerbe der Eskimo und nordamerikänischer Indianer—Berlin.

47. LENORMANT

Essai sur la Propagation de l'alphabet phenician dans l'ancun Monde.
Paris, Vol. 1 (p. 211).

48. LEWIS, THEODORE HAYES

Ancient Rock Inscriptions in Eastern Dakota.
Reprint: American Naturalist, May—1886.
Tracts for Archaeologists: being reprints from various periodicals. 1880-1891 (first series).
Incised Boulders in the Upper Minnesota Valley.
Reprint: American Naturalist, September—1889.
Sculptured rock at Trempelean, Wisconsin.
Reprint: American Naturalist, September—1889.
Copper Mines Worked by the Mound Builders.
Reprint: American Antequarian, September—1889.
Cave-Drawings.
New York—1889.
Reprint: Appleton's Annual Cyclopaedia.
Boulder Outline Figures in the Dakotas, Surveyed in the Summer of 1890.
Reprint: American Anthropologist, January—1891.
Description of some copper relics of the collection of T. H. Lewis in the Macalaster Museum of History and Archaeology.
Reprint: Macalaster College Contributions, No. 6.

49. MACCURDY, GEORGE GRANT

Nature Reflected in the Art of the Ancient Chiriquians.
Reprint: Natural History, Vol. 19, No. 2, (pp. 141-151) 1929.
The Octopus Motive in Ancient Chiriquian Art.
Reprint: American Anthropologist (n. s.) Vol. 18, No. 3 July-September, 1916.

50. MASON, WILLIAM A.

A History of the Art of Writing.
McMillan—1920.

51. MERCER, HENRY CHAPMAN—1856

The Lenape Stone; or, The Indian and the Mammoth.
New York and London. G. P. Putnam Sons—1885.

52. MUSEUM JOURNAL

Issue for March, 1926.

53. OLBRECHTS, FRANS M.

Kunst van Vroeg en van Verre.
Brugge—1929.

54. PARRY, FRANCIS
The Sacred Symbols and Numbers of Aboriginal Americans in Ancient and Modern Times.
Reprint: Bulletin of the American Geographical Society, No. 2—1894.

55. PETROGLYPHS—
American Anthropologist, n. s. Vol. 5, No. 2, April-June.
Page 256, Plate 31—Page 277, Plate 33—Page 279, Plate 34—Page 280.

56. PETROGLYPHS—
Brinton—of Ohio.
In: Proceedings of the Academy of Natural Sciences, Pt. 2, May-October—1884.

57. PETROGLYPHS (CANADA)
Report: Prov. Mus. British Columbia—1925.

58. PICTOGRAPHS—
Dighton Rock.
In: El Palacio, Vol. 26, No. 9-12.
March 2-23-1929. (pp. 174-175).

59. PICTOGRAPHS—
Fewkes, J. Walter.
Prehistoric Porto Rican Pictographs.
In: American Anthropologist, n. s. Vol. 5, No. 3.
July-September, 1903. (p. 441).

60. PUTNAM, F. W.
Conventionalism in Ancient American Art.
Reprint: Bulletin of the Essex Institute, Vol. 18, 1886.
Symbolism in Ancient American Art.
Reprint: Proceedings of the American Association for the Advancement of Science, Vol. 44, 1896.

61. SCHOOL ARTS MAGAZINE
Issue for November, 1927, Vol. 27, No. 3.

62. SCHOOL CRAFT
Indian Tribes of the United States, Vol. I.

63. SMITH, HARLAN I.
Archaeological Reconnaissance in Wyoming, New York—1908.
Excerpt: American Museum Journal, Vol. 8, No. 2, February. (pp. 22-25).

64. SMITH, VICTOR J.
The Human Hand in Primitive Art.
Austin, Texas—1925.

Reprint: Pub. Texas Folk-lore Society (pp. 2-23).
Indian Pictographs of the Big Bend in Texas.
Austin, Texas—1923.
Reprint: Pub. Texas Folk-lore Sox., No. 2 (pp. 2-13).

65. SPECK, FRANK G.
Symbolism in Penobscot Art.
In: Anthropological Papers of the American Museum of Natural History, Vol. 29, Pt. 2-1927.

66. STARR, FREDERICK
Dress and Adornment: Iv. Religious Dress. New York, 1891.
Excerpt: Popular Science Monthly (pp. 194-206) December.

67. STRONG, WILLIAM DUNCAN AND SCHENCK, W. EGBERT
Petroglyphs Near the Dalles of the Columbia River.
Excerpt: American Anthropologist, n. s., Vol. 27, 1925. (pp. 76-90).

68. THE GROWTH OF SYMBOLISM: SYMBOLISM AND THE TOTEM SYSTEM.
In: The American Antiquarian, Vol. 7, No. 6, November 1885. (pp. 321-349).

69. TALMADGE, JAMES E.
The "Michigan relics," a story of forgery and deception.
Salt Lake City. Desent Museum—1911.
Desent Museum Bulletin, n. s., No. 2.

70. THEVENIN, RENE AND COZE, PAUL
Moeurs et histoire des Peaux-Rouge.
Payat, Paris—1928.

71. TOOKER, WILLIAM WALLACE
The Swastika and Other Marks Among the Eastern Algonkians.
Reprint: American Antiquarian, December 1898.

72. TRADITIONAL ART OF THE AMERICAN INDIAN.
Reprint: The American Architect (pp. 537-539).
April 20, 1927.

73. UTZINGER, RUDOLF
Indianer-Kunst. München, 1921.

74. WARDLE, H. NEWELL
Stone Ceremonials in Relation to Algonkian Symbolism.
In: Proceedings of the Academy of Natural Sciences of Philadelphia, Vol. 75, 1923 (pp. 379-391).

75. WESTLAKE, INEZ B.
American Indian Designs. H. C. Perleberg, New York City.

76. WINCHELL, N. H.
Aboriginies of Minnesota. A report based on the collections of Jacob V. Brower, etc., St. Paul, Minnesota. In: Minnesota Historical Society—1911.

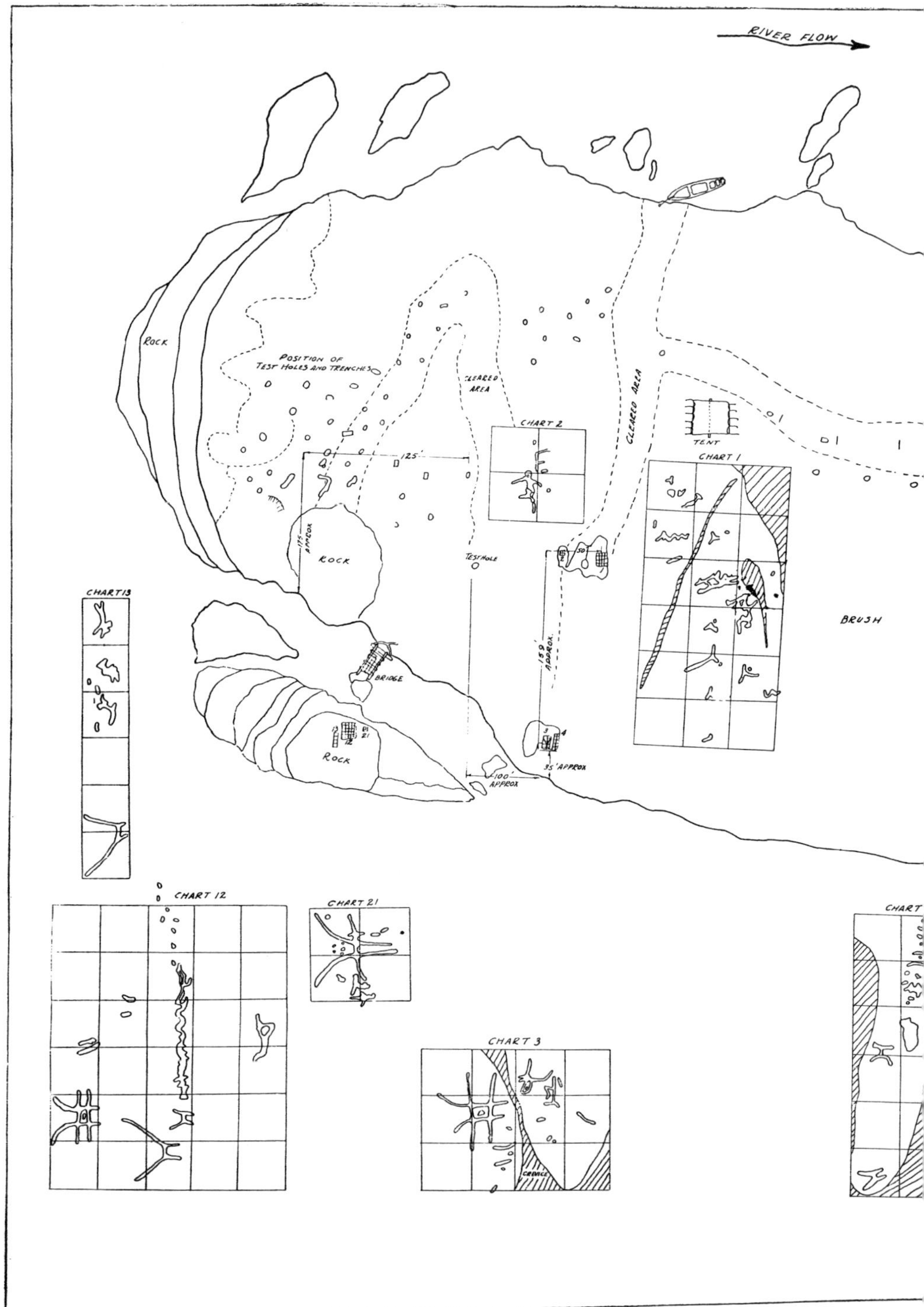

RIVER FLOW
ROCK
POSITION OF
TEST HOLES AND TRENCHES
CLEARED
AREA
CLEARED AREA
CHART 2
TENT
CHART 1
125'
175' APPROX
ROCK
TEST HOLE
BRUSH
159' APPROX.
CHART 13
BRIDGE
ROCK
100' APPROX
35' APPROX
CHART 12
CHART 21
CHART 3
CREVICE
CHART

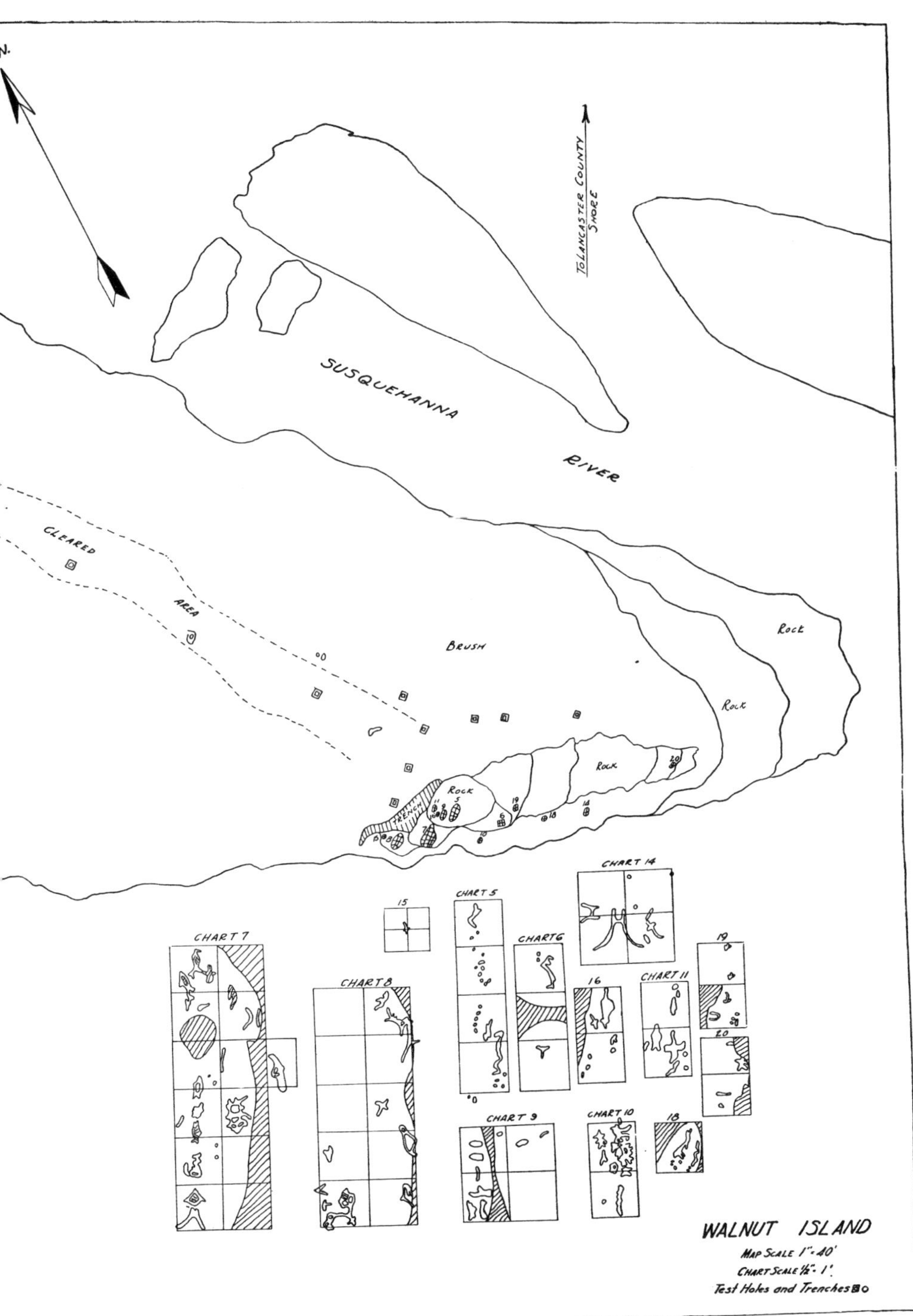
N.
TO LANCASTER COUNTY SHORE
SUSQUEHANNA
RIVER
CLEARED
AREA
BRUSH
Rock
Rock
Rock
Rock
TRENCH
CHART 14
CHART 5
15
CHART 7
CHART 6
CHART 8
16
CHART 11
19
20
CHART 9
CHART 10
18
WALNUT ISLAND
MAP SCALE 1" = 40'
CHART SCALE ½" = 1'
Test Holes and Trenches